TIMES UP

CONNECTING THE DOTS OF BIBLICAL PROPHECY WITH CURRENT WORLD EVENTS

THE WATCHMAN

DARREN J SHIRLEY

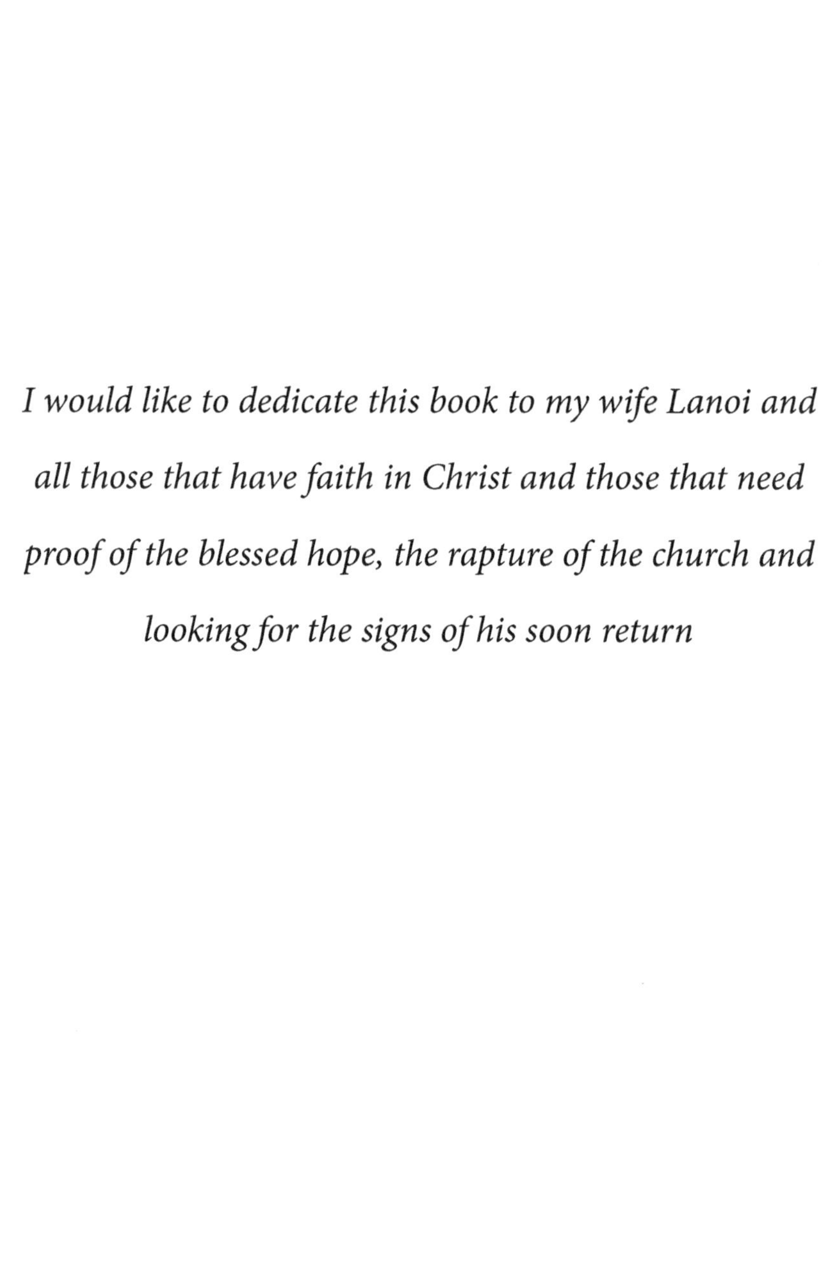

I would like to dedicate this book to my wife Lanoi and
all those that have faith in Christ and those that need
proof of the blessed hope, the rapture of the church and
looking for the signs of his soon return

TABLE OF CONTENTS

WHAT IS THE RAPTURE 1

CHAPTER 1 IS THE RAPTURE REAL.. 5

CHAPTER 2 THE MARRIAGE SUPPER OF THE LAMB 16

CHAPTER 3 CHRISTS SECOND COMING 21

CHAPTER 4 RAPTURE VS SECOND COMING 25

CHAPTER 5 1000 YEAR MILLENNIAL REIGN.. 30

CHAPTER 6 A NEW HEAVEN AND NEW EARTH 34

CHAPTER 7 HOW CLOSE ARE WE TO THE RAPTURE? 37

CHAPTER 8 7000 YEAR SABBATICAL TIMELINE.................................... 68

CHAPTER 9 7 YEAR TRIBULATION 81

CHAPTER 10 THE 7 FEASTS OF ISRAEL.. 86

CHAPTER 11 THE COMING WARS.. 95

CHAPTER 12 THE CONCERN OF CERN 115

CHAPTER 13 THE GREAT RESET 119

CHAPTER 14 MYSTERY BABYLON 133

CHAPTER 15 JESUS IS COMING VERY SOON................................. 143

SO MUCH MORE 148

ABOUT THE AUTHOR.. 151

FINAL THOUGHTS... 152

WHAT IS THE RAPTURE

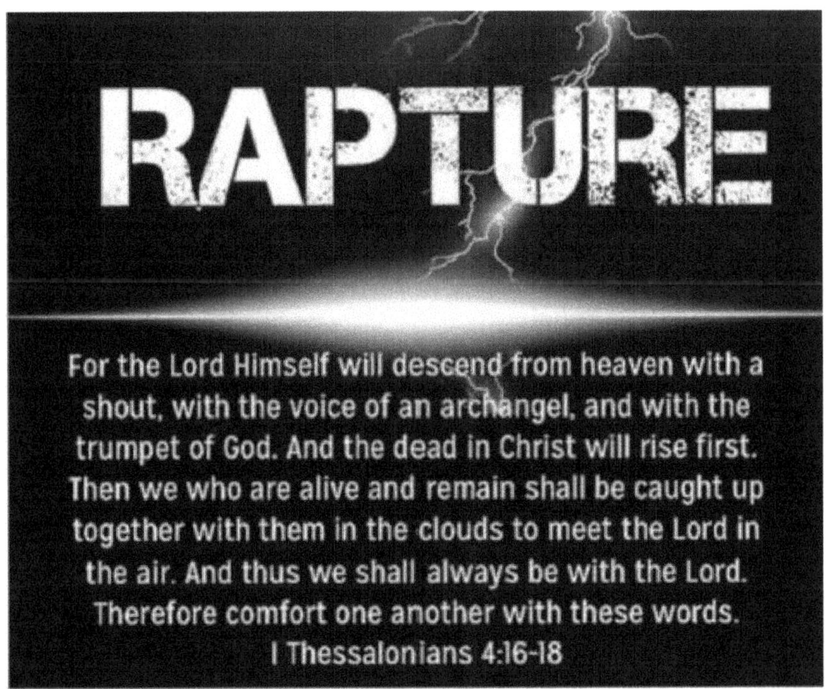

This book is written using dispensational theory.

Dispensationalists hold to a literal interpretation of the Bible as the best hermeneutic. The literal interpretation gives each word the meaning it would commonly have in everyday usage. Allowances are made for symbols, figures of speech, and types, of course. It is understood that even symbols and figurative sayings have literal meanings behind them. So, for example, when the Bible speaks of "a thousand years" in Revelation 20, dispensationalists interpret it as a literal period of 1,000 years (the dispensation of the Kingdom), since there is no compelling reason to interpret it otherwise.

There are at least two reasons why literalism is the best way to view Scripture. First, philosophically, the purpose of language itself requires that we interpret words literally. Language was given by God for the purpose of being able to communicate. Words are vessels of meaning. The second reason is biblical. Every prophecy about Jesus Christ in the Old Testament was fulfilled literally. Jesus' birth, ministry, death, and resurrection all occurred exactly as the Old Testament predicted. The prophecies were literal. There is no non-literal fulfillment of messianic prophecies in the New Testament. This argues strongly for the literal method. If a literal interpretation is not used in studying the Scriptures, there is no objective standard by which to understand the Bible. Each person would be able to interpret the Bible as he saw fit. Biblical interpretation would devolve into "what this passage says to me" instead of "the Bible says." Sadly, this is already the case in much of what is called Bible study today.

Dispensational theology teaches that there are two distinct peoples of God: Israel and the Church. Dispensationalists believe that salvation has always been by grace through faith alone—in God in the Old Testament and specifically in God the Son in the New Testament.

Dispensationalists hold that the Church has not replaced Israel in God's program and that the Old Testament promises to Israel have not been transferred to the Church. Dispensationalism teaches that the promises God made to Israel in the Old Testament (for land, many descendants, and blessings) will be ultimately fulfilled in the 1000-year period spoken of in Revelation 20.

Dispensationalists believe that, just as God is in this age focusing His attention on the Church, He will again in the future focus His attention on Israel (see Romans 9–11 and Daniel 9:24).

Dispensationalists understand the Bible to be organized into seven dispensations: Innocence (Genesis 1:1—3:7), Conscience

(Genesis 3:8—8:22), Human Government

(Genesis 9:1—11:32), Promise (Genesis

12:1—Exodus 19:25), Law (Exodus 20:1— Acts 2:4), Grace (Acts 2:4—Revelation

20:3), and the Millennial Kingdom (Revelation 20:4–6). Again, these dispensations are not paths to salvation, but manners in which God relates to man. Each dispensation includes a recognizable pattern of how God worked with people living in the dispensation. That pattern is 1) a responsibility, 2) a failure, 3) a judgment, and 4) grace to move on.

Dispensationalism, as a system, results in a premillennial interpretation of Christ's second coming and usually a pretribulational interpretation of the rapture. To summarize, dispensationalism is a theological system that emphasizes the literal interpretation of Bible prophecy, recognizes a distinction between Israel and the Church, and organizes the Bible into different dispensations or administrations.

CHAPTER 1

IS THE RAPTURE REAL

"What is the rapture and where is it in the Bible?"

The rapture is our blessed hope. It's Jesus' promise that He would come to gather the church unto Himself before His great wrath is poured out at the end of the age. A question that is often asked is, "Where is the word 'rapture' in the Bible?" Well, it depends on the Bible that you're using. If you're using an English Bible, you won't find the word 'rapture.' The English Bible, however, is a translation from the original Greek, Hebrew, Aramaic, and Latin.

The word 'rapture' comes from the original Greek word 'harpazo,' which

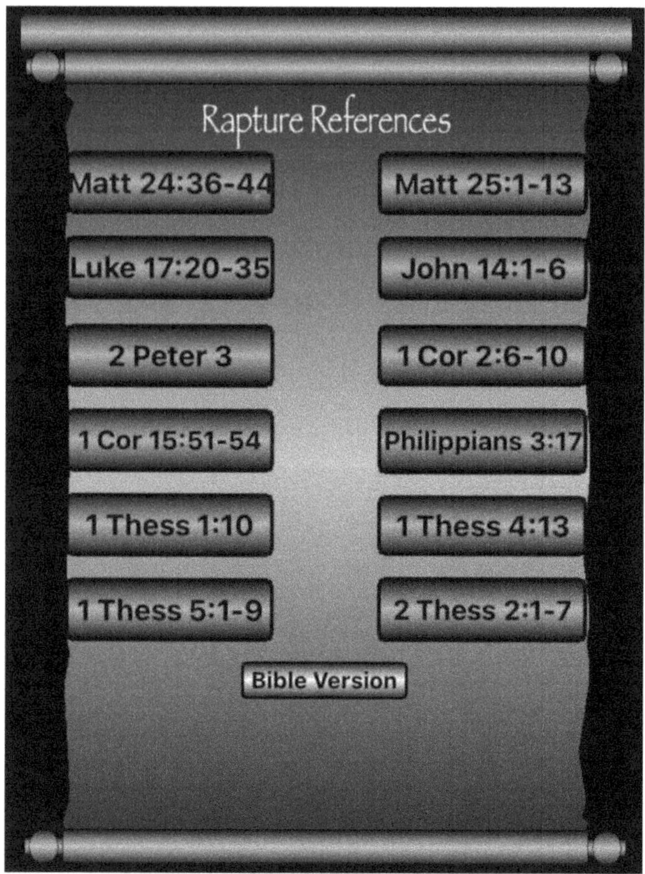

"Means to be caught up or to be snatched away forcefully. In the Latin translation, it is *rapio* or *raptus*, which is where we get the word *Rapture* from. The purpose of the Rapture is to spare the church from God's wrath.

The New Testament emphasizes that believers during the church age are exempt from God's wrath, which will be unleashed during the seven-year tribulation. For instance, 1 Thessalonians 1:10 speaks of

Jesus delivering believers from the coming wrath, and 1 Thessalonians 5:9 states that God has not appointed us to suffer wrath but to receive salvation through Jesus Christ. Titus 2:13 (NIV) states: 'while we wait for the blessed hope—the appearing of the glory of our great God and Savior, Jesus Christ.'

These references further support the notion that the church will not experience the trials of the tribulation and fosters anticipation of Christ's return.

In the Book of Revelation, the term 'church' appears 20 times, with 19 occurrences in the first three chapters. Following that, the church is notably absent from the narrative until Revelation 22:16, raising significant questions about its role during the tribulation period. Specifically, in Revelation 6:2-18, there is a peculiar lack of mention of the church on Earth during this time of great distress. It is intriguing that the scriptures do not provide guidance to believers on how to endure the tribulation, which could be expected if the church were to remain present. This absence may be interpreted as a significant implication, suggesting that the church may not be on Earth during these events.

The most popular rapture verse is 1 Thessalonians 4:13-18 (NIV):

[13] Brothers and sisters, we do not want you to be uninformed about those who sleep in death so that you do not grieve like the rest of mankind, who have no hope. [14] For we believe that Jesus died and rose again, and so we believe that God will bring with Jesus those who have fallen asleep in Him. [15] According to the Lord's word, we tell you that we who are still alive, who are left until the coming of the Lord, will certainly not precede those who have fallen asleep. [16] For the Lord himself will come down from heaven, with a loud command, with the voice of the archangel, and with the trumpet call of God, and the dead in Christ will rise first. [17] After that, we who are still alive and are left will be caught up together with them in the clouds to meet the Lord in the air. And so we will be with the Lord forever. [18] Therefore encourage one another with these words."

1 Thessalonians 2:1-12 (NIV)

[1] Concerning the coming of our Lord Jesus Christ and our being gathered to Him, we ask you, brothers and sisters, [2] not to become easily unsettled or alarmed by the teaching allegedly from us—whether by a prophecy or by word of mouth or by letter—asserting that the day of the Lord has already come. [3] Don't let anyone deceive you in any way, for that day will not come until the rebellion occurs and the man of lawlessness is revealed, the man doomed to destruction. [4] He will

oppose and will exalt himself over everything that is called God or is worshiped so that he sets himself up in God's temple, proclaiming himself to be God. [5] Don't you remember that when I was with you I used to tell you these things? [6] And now you know what is holding him back so that he may be revealed at the proper time. [7] For the secret power of lawlessness is already at work; but the one who now holds it back will continue to do so till he is taken out of the way. [8] And then the lawless one will be revealed, whom the Lord Jesus will overthrow with the breath of His mouth and destroy by the splendor of His coming. [9] The coming of the lawless one will be in accordance with how Satan works. He will use all sorts of displays of power through signs and wonders that serve the lie, [10] and all the ways that wickedness deceives those who are perishing. They perish because they refused to love the truth and so be saved. [11] For this reason, God sends them a powerful delusion so that they will believe the lie [12] and so that all will be condemned who have not believed the truth but have delighted in wickedness.

2nd Thessalonians 5:1-11 (NIV)

[1] Now, brothers and sisters, about times and dates we do not need to write to you, [2] for you know very well that the day of the Lord will come like a thief in the night. [3] While people are saying, *"Peace and safety,"* destruction will come on them suddenly, as labor pains on a

pregnant woman, and they will not escape. [4] But you, brothers and sisters, are not in darkness so that this day should surprise you like a thief. [5] You are all children of the light and children of the day. We do not belong to the night or to the darkness. [6] So then, let us not be like others, who are asleep, but let us be awake and sober. [7] For those who sleep, sleep at night, and those who get drunk, get drunk at night. [8] But since we belong to the day, let us be sober, putting on faith and love as a breastplate, and the hope of salvation as a helmet. [9] For God did not appoint us to suffer wrath but to receive salvation through our Lord Jesus Christ. [10] He died for us so that, whether we are awake or asleep, we may live together with Him. [11] Therefore, encourage one another and build each other up, just as in fact you are doing.

1 Thessalonians 1:10 (NIV)

And to wait for His Son from heaven, whom He raised from the dead—Jesus, who rescues us from the coming wrath.

1 Corinthians 15:51-52 (NIV)

[51] Listen, I tell you a mystery: We will not all sleep, but we will all be changed— [52] in a flash, in the twinkling of an eye, at the last trumpet. For the trumpet will sound, the dead will be raised imperishable, and we will be changed.

Revelation 3:10 (NIV)

"Since you have kept My command to endure patiently, I will also keep you from the hour of trial that is going to come on the whole world to test the inhabitants of the earth."

2 Peter 3:8-10 (NIV)

[8] But do not forget this one thing, dear friends: With the Lord, a day is like a thousand years, and a thousand years are like a day. [9] The Lord is not slow in keeping His promise, as some understand slowness. Instead, He is patient with you, not wanting anyone to perish, but everyone to come to repentance. [10] But the day of the Lord will come like a thief. The heavens will disappear with a roar; the elements will be destroyed by fire, and the earth and everything done in it will be laid bare.

Luke 17:20-36 (NIV)

[20] Once, on being asked by the Pharisees when the kingdom of God would come, Jesus replied, "The coming of the kingdom of God is not something that can be observed, [21] nor will people say, 'Here it is,' or *'There it is,' because the kingdom of God is in your midst.*" [22] Then He said to His disciples, "The time is coming when you will long to see one of the days of the Son of Man, but you will not see it. [23] People will tell you, 'There he is!' or 'Here he is!' Do not go running off after them. [24] For the Son of Man in His day will be like the lightning, which

flashes and lights up the sky from one end to the other. [25] But first He must suffer many things and be rejected by this generation. [26] "Just as it was in the days of Noah, so also will it be in the days of the Son of Man. [27] People were eating, drinking, marrying, and being given in marriage up to the day Noah entered the ark. Then the flood came and destroyed them all. [28] "It was the same in the days of Lot. People were eating and drinking, buying and selling, planting and building. [29] But the day Lot left Sodom, fire and sulfur rained down from heaven and destroyed them all. [30] *It will be just like this on the day the Son of Man is revealed. [31] On that day, no one who is on the housetop, with possessions inside, should go down to get them. Likewise, no one in the field should go back for anything. [32] Remember Lot's wife! [33] Whoever tries to keep their life will lose it, and whoever loses their life will preserve it. [34] I tell you, on that night two people will be in one bed; one will be taken and the other left. [35] Two women will be grinding grain together; one will be taken and the other left." [36]*

Matthew 24:36-44 (NIV)

[36] "But about that day or hour no one knows, not even the angels in heaven, nor the Son, but only the Father. [37] As it was in the days of Noah, so it will be at the coming of the Son of Man. [38] For in the days before the flood, people were eating and drinking, marrying and giving in marriage, up to the day Noah entered the ark; [39] and they

knew nothing about what would happen until the flood came and took them all away. That is how it will be at the coming of the Son of Man. [40] Two men will be in the field; one will be taken and the other left. [41] Two women will be grinding with a hand mill; one will be taken and the other left. [42] "Therefore keep watch, because you do not know on what day your Lord will come. [43] But understand this: If the owner of the house had known at what time of night the thief was coming, he would have kept watch and would not have let his house be broken into. [44] So you also must be ready, because the Son of Man will come at an hour when you do not expect Him.

Matthew 25:1-13 (NIV)

[1] "At that time the kingdom of heaven will be like ten virgins who took their lamps and went out to meet the bridegroom. [2] Five of them were foolish and five were wise. [3] The foolish ones took their lamps but did not take any oil with them. [4] The wise ones, however, took oil in jars along with their lamps. [5] The bridegroom was a long time in coming, and they all became drowsy and fell asleep. [6] "At midnight the cry rang out: 'Here's the bridegroom! Come out to meet him!' [7] "Then all the virgins woke up and trimmed their lamps. [8] The foolish ones said to the wise, 'Give us some of your oil; our lamps are going out.' [9] " 'No,' they replied, 'there may not be enough for both us and you. Instead, go to those who sell oil and buy some for yourselves.' [10]

"But while they were on their way to buy the oil, the bridegroom arrived. The virgins who were ready went in with him to the wedding banquet. And the door was shut. [11] "Later the others also came. 'Lord, Lord,' they said, 'open the door for us!' [12] "But he replied, 'Truly I tell you, I don't know you.' [13] "Therefore keep watch, because you do not know the day or the hour."

John 14:1-4 (NIV)

[1] "Do not let your hearts be troubled. You believe in God; believe also in me. [2] My Father's house has many rooms (mansions); if that were not so, would I have told you that I am going there to prepare a place for you? [3] And if I go and prepare a place for you, I will come back and take you to be with me that you also may be where I am. [4] You know the way to the place where I am going."

You see, Jesus here is clearly talking about the rapture to heaven versus the 2nd coming, where He comes back to earth.

1. Revelation 1:7: This verse states, "*Look, He is coming with the clouds, and every eye will see Him, even those who pierced Him; and all peoples on earth will mourn because of Him. So shall it be! Amen.*" This passage emphasizes the visibility of Christ's return and its significance.

2. Revelation 19:11-16: This section describes the vision of Christ's triumphant return as a warrior. It portrays Him riding a white horse, with the name "Faithful and True," and a sharp sword coming from His mouth to strike down the nations. This passage highlights His authority and the establishment of His reign.

3. Revelation 20:1-6: This part speaks about the thousand-year reign of Christ on Earth, known as the Millennium. It describes the binding of Satan and the reign of Christ with His saints during this period.

CHAPTER 2
THE MARRIAGE SUPPER OF THE
LAMB

Parallel of a Jewish wedding

The very first public miracle Jesus performed took place at a wedding. During the Wedding at Cana, He turned water into wine. Have you ever wondered why He stepped into this public ministry at a wedding? Throughout the New Testament, God's Word makes it clear that the traditions of a 1st-century Jewish wedding align with our relationship with Jesus. The relationship of bride and groom is used in multiple places to describe our relationship with Him, which is why there are multiple parallels between a Jewish wedding and the events of the end times.

The Father's House

In a first-century Jewish wedding, the groom would leave his house and go to the house of his bride. After paying the price for the bride (a dowry known as a *mohar*), the marriage covenant would be established, and the young man and woman would become husband and wife. To symbolize that covenant, they would drink together from a cup of wine. After establishing this covenant, the groom would then leave his bride at her home and return to his father's house. They were still considered to be married but would not live together or consummate the marriage sexually. At this point, the bride and groom would remain separated for around 12 months. During this time of separation, the groom prepared a dwelling place for the bride, typically in his father's house. The groom could not return to get his bride until the father gave him permission.

Watching and Waiting

Meanwhile, the bride was waiting at home, preparing for the return of her groom. She knew generally when he would come back to collect her but didn't know precisely when that would occur—because the father made that decision. As the time drew close, however, she kept lamps burning, just in case. Jesus referenced this tradition when He told the Parable of the Ten Virgins in Matthew 25. It is a parable about being ready to meet Him, even though we know "neither the day nor the hour in which the Son of Man is coming" (Matthew 25:13).

Because the bride didn't know the exact time of her bridegroom's return, his arrival was always preceded by a shout, which announced her imminent departure. With much fanfare, the wedding party would gather as the groom picked up his bride. Then they traveled together to the home of the groom's father.

When the two arrived, they consummated their marriage in the bridal chamber he had prepared. Then they joined the wedding party waiting outside, and everyone would celebrate together for the next seven days.

The Marriage of the Lamb

I hope you see the parallels between this tradition and the prophecies throughout the Bible about the Rapture.

- We have been saved and are presented to Jesus as a pure bride. In 2 Corinthians 11:2, Paul compares this to the betrothal or engagement process: "For I have betrothed you to one husband, that I may present you as a chaste virgin to Christ."

- Jesus has temporarily parted ways with us, to be with His Father. He is preparing a place for us there. "And if I go and prepare a place for you, I will come again and receive you to Myself; that where I am, there you may be also" (John 14:3).

- Jesus said none of us knows the day or the hour of His return. The Son doesn't even know because the timing will be determined by God, the Father.

- Even though we can't predict the exact moment, we do have some idea of when He will return. This is because He encouraged us to keep watch and pay attention to the signs of His return. "Watch therefore, for you do not know what hour your Lord is coming" (Matthew 24:42).

- When the time comes, the Rapture will be announced with a shout, according to 1 Thessalonians 4:16. Paul writes, "For the Lord Himself will descend from heaven with a shout, with the voice of an archangel, and with the trumpet of God."

- The passage in 1 Thessalonians then goes on to say we will be caught up and gathered with Him to "meet the Lord in the air." Then, He will take us to the place He has prepared for us, His Father's house, where we will celebrate.

- The traditional Jewish wedding celebration would last seven days. After the Rapture, the world will experience seven years of tribulation. During that same seven-year period, believers will be celebrating the Wedding Supper of the Lamb.

- The last wedding in human history will be the marriage between God and His people, and it will take place in the New Jerusalem, the holy city, where "God will wipe away every tear from their eyes; there shall be no more death, nor sorrow, nor crying. There shall be no more pain, for the former things have passed away" (Revelation 21:4).

- As we wait for this universe-transforming celebration, we should live in awareness that our Bridegroom is coming soon. We keep ourselves pure and holy. We know He prepares a place for us at His Father's house, so we watch and wait for His return. As the multitude sings in Revelation 19:7, "Let us be glad and rejoice and give Him glory, for the marriage of the Lamb has come, and His wife has made herself ready."

Are you ready?

CHAPTER 3

CHRISTS SECOND COMING

The second coming of Jesus Christ is a fundamental doctrine in Christianity, signifying the anticipated return of the Son of God to Earth. This chapter seeks to examine the second coming in depth, focusing on its scriptural foundations, theological significance, and the key events expected to unfold during this extraordinary occasion. By exploring these elements, we can enhance our understanding of the profound and transformative implications of the second coming.

Scriptural Foundations

The idea of the second coming is firmly rooted in numerous biblical passages that affirm the promise of Christ's return. For instance, in Acts 1:11, as Jesus ascended into heaven, two angels proclaimed to the disciples, "This same Jesus, who has been taken from you into heaven, will come back in the same way you have seen Him go into heaven." This statement establishes the certainty of Christ's return and lays the groundwork for further teachings on the topic.

Additional passages, such as Matthew 24:30, 1 Thessalonians 4:16, and Revelation 1:7, further reinforce the assurance of Christ's second coming. These scriptures illustrate the magnificent nature of this event, emphasizing the visible and glorious return of Jesus to reclaim His creation, judge the living and the dead, and establish His eternal kingdom.

Theological Significance

The second coming carries immense theological importance within Christian belief systems. It marks the culmination of God's redemptive plan, signifying the ultimate victory over sin, evil, and death. This event exemplifies the fullest expression of God's justice, mercy, and love, bringing about the fulfillment of His divine purposes for humanity and creation.

Moreover, the second coming signifies the realization of prophecies found in both the Old and New Testaments. The return of Jesus affirms the reliability of God's Word, reinforcing the divine authority and trustworthiness of Scripture. Additionally, it highlights the reality of resurrection and the promise of eternal life, providing hope and assurance to believers in the face of earthly trials and tribulations.

Anticipated Events

The second coming of Jesus Christ involves several anticipated events, each carrying significant theological and eschatological implications. These events encompass the resurrection of the dead, the Rapture of the church, the judgment of all people, the defeat of evil forces, and the establishment of Christ's eternal kingdom, during which the saints will assume positions of authority.

The resurrection of the dead is a central feature of the second coming, as Christ will raise both the righteous and the unrighteous for judgment. Believers will experience a bodily resurrection during the Rapture, receiving glorified bodies and eternal life, while those who rejected Him will face eternal separation from God.

The Rapture, as outlined in 1 Thessalonians 4:17, refers to the immediate gathering of believers to meet Christ in the air. This event precedes the tribulation period, during which God will pour out His wrath on the earth. The Rapture serves as a means of deliverance for believers, shielding them from impending judgment.

Additionally, the second coming encompasses the judgment of all people. In Matthew 25:31-46, Jesus illustrates the separation of the sheep (believers) from the goats (unbelievers) during the final judgment. This divine assessment will determine individuals' responses to the message of salvation and their treatment of others, emphasizing the significance of faith and good works.

The saints will not only participate in this momentous event but will also be granted positions of authority, ruling and reigning with Christ for a thousand years. This period, known as the Millennium, will see believers entrusted with governance over various aspects of creation, reflecting their faithfulness and service during their earthly lives.

Conclusion

The second coming of Jesus Christ is a pivotal event with profound implications for believers and the world at large. Its scriptural basis, theological significance, and anticipated events all contribute to the transformative essence of this future occurrence. As Christians, we eagerly await the return of our Savior, recognizing the hope, redemption, and eternal life that will be fully realized in His glorious second coming. May we continue to live in anticipation, faithfully serving God and sharing His love until that day arrives.

CHAPTER 4
RAPTURE VS SECOND COMING

The concepts of the Rapture and the Second Coming of Christ are pivotal in Christian eschatology, representing two distinct events that are often confused or conflated. Understanding the differences between these two occurrences is essential for a comprehensive grasp of biblical prophecy and the future of the Church. This chapter explores the key distinctions between the Rapture, where the Church meets the Lord in the air before the tribulation, and the Second Coming, when Christ returns to earth after the seven-year tribulation.

Definitions and Timing

The **Rapture** is the event in which believers in Christ are taken up from the earth to meet the Lord in the air. This event is typically understood to occur before the Great Tribulation, a period of intense suffering and judgment described in the Book of Revelation. The primary biblical text associated with the Rapture is 1 Thessalonians 4:16-17, which describes how the dead in Christ will rise first, followed by living believers who will be caught up to meet the Lord.

The **Second Coming**, on the other hand, refers to Christ's return to earth at the end of the tribulation period. This event is characterized by Jesus' physical return to establish His kingdom and execute judgment. Key passages that describe the Second Coming include Revelation 19:11-16, which depicts Christ returning as a conquering King, and Matthew 24:30-31, where the Son of Man appears in the sky and sends His angels to gather the elect.

Purpose and Nature of the Events

The purpose of the Rapture is primarily to rescue the Church from the impending wrath of God that will be poured out during the tribulation. It serves as a promise of hope for believers, affirming that God will not subject His faithful followers to the trials that are to come. The Rapture is often described as a moment of joy and celebration, where believers are united with Christ and with one another.

In contrast, the Second Coming serves a dual purpose: to fulfill the prophetic promises made to Israel and to judge the nations. This event signifies the culmination of God's redemptive plan and His establishment of a millennial kingdom on earth. Unlike the Rapture, which is characterized by a private meeting with Christ in the air, the Second Coming is public and visible to all, as described in Revelation 1:7, which states that every eye will see Him.

Participants

The participants in the Rapture are exclusively believers in Christ—those who have accepted Him as Lord and Savior, whether dead or alive. This event underscores the Church's unique relationship with Christ and emphasizes the grace extended to believers.

Conversely, the Second Coming involves not only the redeemed but also the unredeemed. At this time, Christ will return to judge the living and the dead. The righteous will be rewarded and enter into the millennial kingdom, while the unrighteous will face judgment and condemnation.

Biblical Evidence and Interpretations

Several passages are cited to support the doctrine of the Rapture. In addition to 1 Thessalonians 4:16-17, John 14:1-3 is often referenced, where Jesus promises to prepare a place for His followers and come again to receive them. The interpretation of these scriptures supports the view that the Rapture will occur before the tribulation.

For the Second Coming, numerous Old Testament prophecies, such as Zechariah 14:4, describe the Messiah's return to the Mount of Olives. In the New Testament, passages like Matthew 24 and Revelation 19 further elaborate on the nature and significance of Christ's return after the tribulation.

Theological Implications

The distinction between the Rapture and the Second Coming carries significant theological implications. The belief in the Rapture highlights the Church's hope and expectation of Christ's imminent return, encouraging believers to live in a state of readiness and anticipation. It emphasizes grace and deliverance from judgment.

In contrast, the Second Coming focuses on the fulfillment of God's promises to Israel, the establishment of His kingdom, and the ultimate triumph of good over evil. This event serves as a reminder of God's sovereignty and justice in the world, as well as the accountability of all humanity before Him.

Conclusion

In summary, the Rapture of the Church and the Second Coming of Christ represent two distinct events in Christian eschatological teaching. The Rapture signifies the Church's meeting with Christ in the air prior to the tribulation, serving as a promise of salvation and hope for believers. The Second Coming, however, marks Christ's triumphant return to earth after the tribulation, fulfilling God's promises and executing divine judgment. Understanding these differences not only clarifies biblical prophecy but also enriches the faith and hope of believers as they navigate the challenges of the present.

CHAPTER 5

1000 YEAR MILLENNIAL REIGN

The concept of the thousand-year millennial reign of Jesus Christ is primarily rooted in the Book of Revelation, but there are several other verses throughout the Bible that are associated with this theme. Below are key verses that reference or imply the millennial reign:

Key Verses in Revelation

1. Revelation 20:1-6 (NIV)

And I saw an angel coming down out of heaven, having the key to the Abyss and holding in his hand a great chain. He seized the dragon, that ancient serpent, who is the devil, and bound him for a thousand years. He threw him into the Abyss, and locked and sealed it over him, to keep him from deceiving the nations anymore until the thousand years were ended. After that, he must be set free for a short time.

I saw thrones on which were seated those (the church) who had been given authority to judge. And I saw the souls of those who had been beheaded because of their testimony about Jesus and because of the word of God. They had not worshiped the beast or its image and had not received its mark on their foreheads or their hands. They came to life and reigned with Christ a thousand years. (The rest of the dead did not come to life until the thousand years were ended.) This is the first resurrection.

Blessed and holy are those who share in the first resurrection. The second death has no power over them, but they will be priests of God and of Christ and will reign with him for a thousand years."

Old Testament References

2. Isaiah 2:2-4 (NIV)

"In the last days, the mountain of the Lord's temple will be established as the highest of the mountains; it will be exalted above the hills, and all nations will stream to it. Many peoples will come and say, 'Come, let us go up to the mountain of the Lord, to the temple of the God of Jacob. He will teach us his ways, so that we may walk in his paths.' The law will go out from Zion, the word of the Lord from Jerusalem. He will judge between the nations and will settle disputes for many peoples. They will beat their swords into plowshares and their spears into pruning hooks. Nation will not take up sword against nation, nor will they train for war anymore."

3. Isaiah 11:6-9 (NIV)

"The wolf will live with the lamb, the leopard will lie down with the goat, the calf and the lion and the yearling together; and a little child will lead them. The cow will feed with the bear, their young will lie down together, and the lion will eat straw like the ox. The infant will play near the cobra's den, and the young child will put its hand into the viper's nest. They will neither harm nor destroy on all my holy mountain, for the earth will be filled with the knowledge of the Lord as the waters cover the sea."

4.   Jeremiah 23:5-6 (NIV)

"The days are coming, declares the Lord, when I will raise up for David a righteous Branch, a King who will reign wisely and do what is just and right in the land. In his days Judah will be saved and Israel will live in safety. This is the name by which he will be called: The Lord Our Righteous Savior."

5.   5.Ezekiel 37:24-25 (NIV)

"My servant David will be king over them, and they will all have one shepherd. They will follow my laws and be careful to keep my decrees. They will live in the land I gave to my servant Jacob, the land where your ancestors lived. They and their children and their children's children will live there forever, and David my servant will be their prince forever."

6.   Matthew 19:28 (NIV)

"Jesus said to them, 'Truly I tell you, at the renewal of all things, when the Son of Man sits on his glorious throne, you who have followed me will also sit on twelve thrones, judging the twelve tribes of Israel.'"

7.   Luke 1:32-33 (NIV)

"He will be great and will be called the Son of the Most High. The Lord God will give him the throne of his father David, and he will reign over Jacob's descendants forever; his kingdom will never end."

These verses collectively contribute to the understanding of the millennial reign of Christ, illustrating peace, righteousness, and divine governance for 1,000 years.

CHAPTER 6

A NEW HEAVEN AND NEW EARTH

The concept of a new heaven and a new earth is primarily found in the Book of Revelation, but it is also alluded to in other parts of the Bible. Here are key verses that discuss the new heaven and the new earth:

Key Verses in Revelation

1. Revelation 21:1-4 (NIV)

"Then I saw a new heaven and a new earth, for the first heaven and the first earth had passed away, and there was no longer any sea. I saw the Holy City, the new Jerusalem, coming down out of heaven from God, prepared as a bride beautifully dressed for her husband. And I heard a loud voice from the throne saying, 'Look! God's dwelling place is now among the people, and He will dwell with them. They will be His people, and God Himself will be with them and be their God. He will wipe every tear from their eyes. There will be no more death or mourning or crying or pain, for the old order of things has passed away.'"

2.   Revelation 21:5-7 (NIV)

"He who was seated on the throne said, 'I am making everything new!' Then He said, 'Write this down, for these words are trustworthy and true.' He said to me: 'It is done. I am the Alpha and the Omega, the Beginning and the End. To the thirsty I will give water without cost from the spring of the water of life. Those who are victorious will inherit all this, and I will be their God and they will be my children.'"

Old Testament References

3.   Isaiah 65:17 (NIV)

"See, I will create new heavens and a new earth. The former things will not be remembered, nor will they come to mind."

4.   Isaiah 66:22 (NIV)

"'As the new heavens and the new earth that I make will endure before me,' declares the Lord, 'so will your name and descendants endure.'"

New Testament Reference

5.   2 Peter 3:13 (NIV)

"But in keeping with His promise, we are looking forward to a new heaven and a new earth, where righteousness dwells."

These verses together depict the hope and promise of a transformed creation, where God will dwell with His people, and all former sorrows will be wiped away.

CHAPTER 7

HOW CLOSE ARE WE TO THE RAPTURE?

What is happening in our world? It appears that society has lost its way. Many individuals seem to have abandoned fundamental morals and family values, believing that children can determine their own gender and that laws are inconsequential. The prevailing woke culture suggests that feelings dictate reality, and if someone feels a certain way, it is deemed acceptable. The LGBTQ+++ community is literally trying to redefine God's creation. Meanwhile, we are faced with wars, economic downturns, and a general search for answers. When we examine current events through the lens of biblical prophecy, it becomes increasingly evident that we are living in the final days—perhaps even the final hours or minutes. Personally, if I were aware that Christ was returning this year, I would strive to make it my most meaningful year. This realization has inspired me to write this book, aimed at reaching those who are open to understanding the signs of the times.

What would you do?

Since 2020, I have been seriously anticipating the rapture. I knew that COVID-19 was a "PLANdemic." I saw right through it. I've done a ton of research to prove it was all planned by the globalists who want to create a New World Order—a one-world government, one-world currency, and one-world religion. I knew with an evil scam so big that it encompasses the whole world, the tribulation couldn't be far off.

So, I started doing a ton of research over the past four years. I suggest you do your own research as well. I'm not going to go into all the proof that COVID was a "scamdemic" in this book. In later chapters, we won't cover all the details, but we will explore enough to connect the dots between what we see happening today and biblical prophecy. I recommend watching the documentary *Plandemic* on uncensored platforms like Rumble, because if all you watch is mainstream media, you have...

been brainwashed in a way because the globalists own all the big networks and control the narrative.

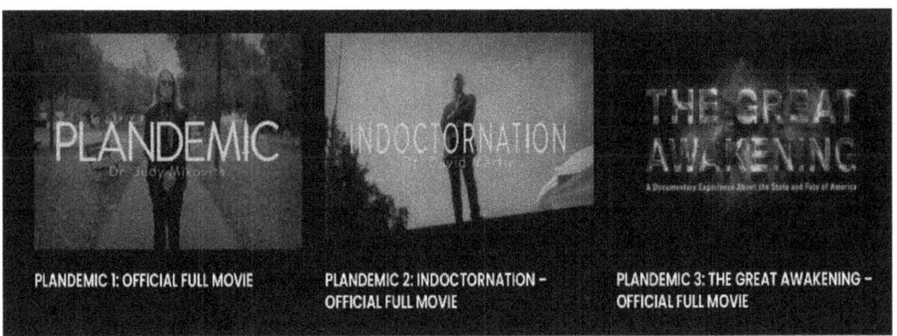

We are the only generation that has the super sign, which is the rebirth of Israel in 1948

We are the only generation that has the "super sign," which is the rebirth of Israel in 1948. One significant world event that aligns with biblical prophecy is the rebirth of Israel as a nation. The restoration of Israel is seen by many scholars as a fulfillment of biblical prophecies, such as Ezekiel 37:21-22, which foretells the gathering of the dispersed Israelites from the nations. This event holds great significance in eschatological discussions, as it sets the stage for other prophetic events to unfold.

Parable of the Fig Tree

And He told them a parable: "Look at the fig tree, and all the trees; as soon as they come out in leaf, you see for yourselves and know that summer is already near. So also, when you see these things taking place, you know that the kingdom of God is near. Truly, I say to you, this generation will not pass away until all has taken place. Heaven and earth will pass away, but my words will not pass away." — Luke 21:29–33

How long is a generation?

The Bible says in Psalm 90:10:

> *"As for the days of our life, they contain seventy years,*
>
> *Or if due to strength, eighty years."*

2024 is Israel's 76th birthday.

In the Olivet Discourse, Jesus gives a lot of detail about what it will be like in the end times.

Matthew 24:3-8 (NIV)

As Jesus was sitting on the Mount of Olives, the disciples came to Him privately. "Tell us, "They said, "when will this happen, and what will be the sign of Your coming and of the end of the age?"

Jesus answered: "Watch out that no one deceives you.

For many will come in my name, claiming, 'I am the Messiah,' and will deceive many.

You will hear of wars and rumors of wars but see to it that you are not alarmed. Such things must happen, but the end is still to come.

Nation will rise against nation, and kingdom against kingdom. There will be famines and earthquakes in various places.

[8] *All these are the beginning of birth pains."*

Timothy 3:1-5 (NIV)

1. But mark this: There will be terrible times in the last days.

2. People will be lovers of themselves, lovers of money, boastful, proud, abusive, disobedient to their parents, ungrateful, unholy

3. without love, unforgiving, slanderous, without self-control, brutal, not lovers of the good,

4. treacherous, rash, conceited, lovers of pleasure rather than lovers of God—

5. having a form of godliness but denying its power. Have nothing to do with such people."

Does this not sound like today's liberal society in the Western world? They have abandoned God's commands and turned toward evil ideology with the new woke culture and Diversity, Equity, and Inclusion (DEI). This culture no longer believes in law; now it's all about how you feel. If a man wants to be a woman, he can identify as one whether he has a sex change or not, and the same goes for women. They have all these new pronouns that they insist you call them; otherwise, they rebel, protest, and even try to get the police involved. They are brainwashing children from the time they are born, teaching them that they don't know what their gender is until they get older. In some states and countries, it's legal to get a sex change as young as 12 years old. Schools are even calling the police to strip away children from their parents if they refuse to put them on puberty blockers.

The LGBTQ+++ list keeps growing as they insist there are more genders all the time. You saw the complete perversion of Jesus Christ at the Paris Olympics this year when they mocked The Last Supper...

with a bunch of transvestites, lesbians, and queers. The closing ceremony was completely satanic and portrayed the Antichrist coming on a white horse.

God's law from the beginning is literally being spit on, as we see in Genesis 2:24:

"Therefore, a man shall leave his father and mother and be joined to his wife, and they shall become one flesh."

The Bible addresses the topic of homosexuality in several passages. One of the most commonly referenced verses is 1 Corinthians 6:9-10, which states:

"Or do you not know that the unrighteous will not inherit the kingdom of God? Do not be deceived: neither the sexually immoral, nor idolaters, nor adulterers, nor men who practice homosexuality, nor thieves, nor the greedy, nor drunkards, nor slanderers, nor swindlers will inherit the kingdom of God."

Another passage is found in Galatians 5:19-21, where Paul lists the acts of the flesh, including sexual immorality, and warns that those who practice such things will not inherit the kingdom of God.

The fact that this ideology is being taught to children at ages before they even know what sex is, is a complete rebellion against God. Matthew 18:6 reads:

"But whoever causes one of these little ones who believe in me to sin, it would be better for him to have a great millstone fastened around his

neck and to be drowned in the depth of the sea." This verse emphasizes the seriousness of leading children or vulnerable individuals away from faith and righteousness, highlighting the severe consequences of such actions. It underscores the importance of protecting and nurturing the faith of the innocent.

Revelation 6:2 states:

"And I looked, and behold, a white horse! The one sitting on it had a bow, and a crown was given to him, and he came out conquering, and to conquer." The world today is literally mocking God. This ideology is satanic at the core and embodies the spirit of the Antichrist. The term *"spirit of Antichrist"* is specifically mentioned in 1 John 4:3, which states:

"And every spirit that does not confess Jesus is not from God. This is the spirit of the Antichrist, which you heard was coming and now is in the world already."

Additionally, in 1 John 2:18, it refers to the Antichrist and mentions that there are many antichrists:

"Children, it is the last hour, and as you have heard that the Antichrist is coming, so now many antichrists have come. Therefore we know that it is the last hour."

What we are seeing today is complete lawlessness.

1. Matthew 7:23: In this verse, Jesus speaks of those who perform miracles in His name but are ultimately rejected because they practice lawlessness.

2. 2 Thessalonians 2:7:** The Apostle Paul refers to the "mystery of lawlessness" that is already at work, indicating a spirit of rebellion against God's law before the coming of the lawless one (often interpreted as the Antichrist).

An Increase in Earthquakes

In Matthew 24, Jesus also talked about an increase in earthquakes as another end times sign.

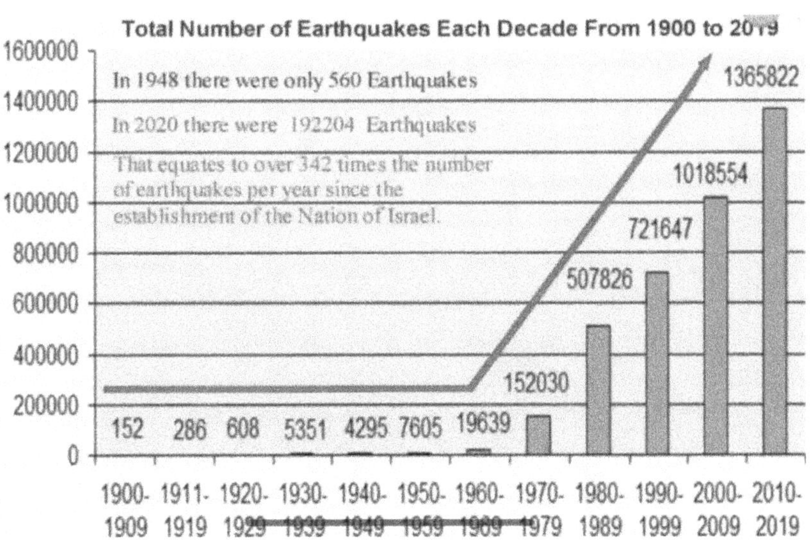

As we can see with this chart, earthquakes have increased dramatically since the rebirth of Israel in 1948. In Matthew 24, Jesus also talked about wars and rumors of wars as another end-times sign. Here are just a few to mention:

1. **Syria** - The civil war continues with various factions involved.

2. **Yemen** - A civil war and humanitarian crisis with ongoing conflict between the Houthis and the Saudi-led coalition.

3. **Ukraine** - The war with Russia has escalated significantly since the invasion in 2022.

4. **Israel/Palestine** - Ongoing tensions and violence, particularly between Israel and Hamas in Gaza and now Hezbollah in Lebanon, with Iran financing all of it.

5. **Afghanistan** - Continued violence and instability following the Taliban's takeover.

6. **Ethiopia** - The conflict in the Tigray region continues, along with ethnic violence in other areas.

7. **Myanmar** - Ongoing conflict following the military coup in 2021, with various ethnic groups and pro-democracy forces fighting against the military junta.

8. **India/Pakistan** - Ongoing tensions, particularly in the Kashmir region, with sporadic violence and military confrontations.

9. **Philippine**s - Ongoing conflict with various insurgent groups, including Abu Sayyaf and communist rebels.

10. **South China Sea** - Territorial disputes and military tensions, particularly involving China and Taiwan, the Philippines, Vietnam, and other nations.

The main war actors on the stage today are Russia and Ukraine, and Israel and Iran, along with their proxies (Hamas, Hezbollah, PA, Houthis in Yemen). The Russia-Ukraine war is by far the largest, with estimates now of around 700,000 Ukrainians dead. They are literally running out of people. You'll never hear this on mainstream media, of course, because the globalists that have penetrated the West and control the United States government and NATO see Putin as a threat to their hegemony and their plans for the New World Order (NWO). The war in Ukraine actually started in 2014 but didn't escalate until 2022 when Russia went into Ukraine to stop the military buildup and production of chemical warfare factories on their border.

Ukraine is arguably the most corrupt country on earth. It is used as a child trafficking tool, as well as a huge money laundering machine.

According to state.gov, the US has sent Ukraine over $55 billion since 2022. That's $170,000 for every US citizen. It's pure theft by robbing the country and sending it to Ukraine to wash the money and then send it back to the globalists who control the United States of America behind the scenes. The rich get richer, and the poor get poorer.

Now the World Economic Forum (WEF), which we will get into more detail about later, is at the forefront of creating the NWO. The World Economic Forum's plan to crush the middle class has been exposed by Putin in Russia. The reason they fear Putin is because he controls the gas pump. He's pointing out the failures of the WEF's energy policies. "The Great Reset" has become a total failure, and now they're getting desperate. Putin's advance into Ukraine was to expose the WEF agenda of destroying the middle class. The WEF's 2030 agenda of "building back better" means they have to destroy the current system in order to build back their own tyrannical top-down control system that will monitor everyone on the planet in whatever they do. They can't let Putin win, or it would disrupt "The Great Reset" and derail "Agenda 2030."

Putin sees the decline of the US dollar and officially headed up the establishment known as the BRICS nations in 2009. BRICS stands for Brazil, Russia, India, China, and South Africa. There are reportedly over 100 countries that have applied to join the BRICS nations. One of their goals is to create a new world reserve currency backed by commodities. Recently, Saudi Arabia just ended its 50-year Petro-dollar agreement with the United States, and they are seeking to join the BRICS nations. This could mean a dramatic decline in the value of the dollar since it is only backed by debt, currently at $35 trillion, and thus would lead to a rapid transition out of the dollar into the new reserve currency. This has the globalists panicking as their plan to control the world becomes uncertain.

Why else would the US keep sending billions of dollars to Ukraine, along with military equipment, missiles, and F-35 jets, with all of NATO and US boots on the ground for a country that has already lost the war? It makes no sense unless you peel back the layers and see the big picture. It's all about a power struggle between the globalists and Russia, with China on their side. Putin has activated his nuclear arsenal, which is the largest in the world, and he's getting ready to use it. It's absolutely insane what is going on there.

The second largest conflict is between Israel and Iran. The Islamic Republic of Iran, established in 1979, has maintained a consistent ideological and military stance toward Israel, which it considers an existential threat. This animosity is rooted in a complex mix of historical grievances, religious ideology, geopolitical strategy, and revolutionary fervor. The regime's declared goal of "wiping Israel off the map" reflects not only a commitment to its revolutionary ideals but also a broader ambition to reshape the political landscape of the Middle East.

Revolutionary Ideology: The foundation of the Iranian regime's hostility toward Israel can be traced back to its revolutionary ideology. The 1979 Islamic Revolution, led by Ayatollah Ruhollah Khomeini, sought to establish a government based on Islamic principles and to oppose Western influence in the region. Khomeini framed Israel as a puppet of Western imperialism, particularly the United States, which had supported the Shah's regime prior to the revolution.

Iran's leadership, primarily composed of Shiite clerics, views the Israeli state through a religious lens. The regime often portrays the Israeli-Palestinian conflict as a struggle between Islam and its enemies, framing the fight against Israel as a religious duty. This narrative resonates deeply with many in the Muslim world, particularly among Shiite communities, and serves to justify Iran's support for militant groups opposing Israel.

Iranian leaders have consistently articulated their opposition to Zionism, which they regard as a colonialist ideology. This opposition is not merely political; it is deeply ideological and theological, positioning Israel as an embodiment of oppression against Muslims and Palestinians. This perspective is propagated through state-controlled media, educational institutions, and religious sermons, reinforcing the notion that the elimination of Israel is a legitimate goal.

Iran has positioned itself as a champion of the Palestinian cause, providing military, financial, and political support to groups such as Hamas and Islamic Jihad. This support is framed as part of a broader Islamic struggle against oppression, and Iran's leaders often invoke the plight of the Palestinian people to rally domestic and regional support.

Iran employs a strategy of asymmetric warfare, utilizing proxy groups to extend its influence and conduct operations against Israel. Groups like Hezbollah in Lebanon and various Palestinian factions in Gaza serve as front-line forces in Iran's confrontation with Israel. This allows Iran to strike at Israel indirectly while maintaining plausible deniability.

Iran has invested heavily in its missile program, viewing it as a crucial component of its military strategy against Israel. The development of precision-guided missiles enhances Iran's capability to threaten Israeli territory directly. Iranian officials openly discuss their missile capabilities as a deterrent, reiterating their commitment to targeting Israel if necessary.

Iran has sought to build alliances with other anti-Israel regimes and non-state actors in the region. By fostering relations with Syria,

Hezbollah, and various Palestinian factions, Iran aims to create a united front against Israel. This network enhances its military capabilities and allows for coordinated attacks, increasing the threat to Israeli security.

In addition to conventional military strategies, Iran has increasingly turned to cyber warfare as a means of undermining Israel. Iranian cyber operations have targeted Israeli infrastructure, financial institutions, and military systems, reflecting a modern approach to conflict that complements traditional military strategies.

Iran's goal of eliminating Israel has significant implications for regional stability. Its actions contribute to ongoing conflicts in Lebanon, Syria, and Gaza, perpetuating cycles of violence and retaliation. The presence of Iranian-backed militias near Israel's borders raises the risk of direct confrontations, complicating peace efforts in the region.

The Iranian threat has prompted the U.S. and Israel to strengthen their military and intelligence cooperation. The two nations have engaged in joint military exercises, enhanced missile defense systems, and increased intelligence sharing to counter Iran's influence. This cooperation reflects a broader strategy to contain Iran and prevent its nuclear ambitions from materializing.

Iran's pursuit of nuclear technology has raised concerns in Israel and the international community. While Iran insists its nuclear program is for peaceful purposes, its leaders have made statements that suggest a willingness to use nuclear capabilities against Israel. The potential for a nuclear-armed Iran significantly alters the strategic balance in the region and escalates tensions.

Iran's ideological commitment to eliminating Israel also complicates the Palestinian struggle for statehood. While Iran supports Palestinian factions, its ultimate goal is not necessarily the establishment of a Palestinian state but rather the destruction of Israel. This dynamic can undermine moderate Palestinian leadership and complicate peace negotiations.

The Iranian regime's ideological and military goals regarding Israel are deeply rooted in a complex interplay of revolutionary ideology, religious fervor, and geopolitical strategy. Iran's commitment to "wiping Israel off the map" is reflected in its support for militant proxies, missile development, and asymmetric warfare strategies. The implications of this stance extend beyond Israel, contributing to regional instability and complicating efforts for peace in the Middle East. As Iran continues to pursue its objectives, the potential for conflict remains high, necessitating vigilance and strategic responses from Israel and its allies. Addressing these ideological and military aspirations will require not only military preparedness but also nuanced diplomatic engagement to mitigate the risks of escalation.

The Falling Away

Another end-times prophecy is the falling away of Christians from the faith. 2 Thessalonians 2:3-4 (NIV) says:

"Don't let anyone deceive you in any way, for that day will not come until the rebellion occurs and the man of lawlessness is revealed, the man doomed to destruction. He will oppose and will exalt himself over everything that is called God or is worshiped, so that he sets himself up in God's temple, proclaiming himself to be God."

In this context, "the rebellion" or "falling away" refers to a significant departure from the faith or a widespread apostasy among believers. Paul emphasizes that this event must happen before the revelation of the Antichrist figure, often referred to as the "man of lawlessness." We are seeing this today with many churches abandoning true scripture and accepting the woke culture, as well as prosperity preaching.

In Matthew 24, Jesus talked about two men being in the field; one will be taken and the other left. Two women will be grinding with a hand mill; one will be taken and the other left. I believe this refers to half of the church departing from the faith. With the world population at around 8 billion, there are approximately just over 2 billion Christians in the world today, so likely around 1 billion of the saints will get raptured, leaving approximately 7 billion to start the tribulation.

The Days of Noah

Matthew 24:36-39 (NIV):

"But about that day or hour no one knows, not even the angels in heaven, nor the Son, but only the Father. As it was in the days of Noah, so it will be at the coming of the Son of Man. For in the days before the flood, people were eating and drinking, marrying and giving in marriage, up to the day Noah entered the ark; and they knew nothing

about what would happen until the flood came and took them all away.

That is how it will be at the coming of the Son of Man."

Knowledge Shall Be Increased

Daniel 12:4 (NIV):

"But you, Daniel, close up and seal the words of the scroll until the time

of the end. Many will go here and there to increase knowledge."

In this context, the verse suggests that in the time of the end, there will be an increase in travel and knowledge.

1. Pre-Industrial Era (Before the 19th Century): For most of human history, knowledge accumulation was slow. It is estimated that knowledge doubled approximately every few centuries. The invention of the printing press in the 15th century began to accelerate the dissemination of knowledge.

2. 19th Century: With the Industrial Revolution, knowledge began to grow more rapidly. The doubling time started to shorten, with estimates suggesting knowledge doubled approximately every 50 years by the end of the 19th century.

3. 20th Century: The advent of computers and the internet further accelerated the pace of knowledge accumulation. By

the mid-20th century, knowledge was estimated to be doubling every 10 to 15 years.

4. 21st Century: In recent years, especially with the rise of digital technology and the internet, some estimates suggest that knowledge is now doubling at an unprecedented rate, potentially every 12 to 18 months. IBM has even suggested that with the growth of big data, such as cloud computing, machine learning, and artificial intelligence, knowledge could be doubling every few hours.

Signs in the Sun, Moon, and Stars

Jesus speaks about signs in the heavens, including the sun and the moon, in the Gospel of Luke. Specifically, Luke 21:25-26 states:

"And there will be signs in the sun, in the moon, and in the stars; and on the earth distress of nations, with perplexity, the sea and the waves roaring; men's hearts failing them from fear and the expectation of those things which are coming on the earth, for the powers of the heavens will be shaken."

Additionally, in Matthew 24:29-30, Jesus mentions signs in the heavens related to His second coming:

"Immediately after the tribulation of those days, the sun will be darkened, and the moon will not give its light; the stars will fall from heaven, and the powers of the heavens will be shaken. Then the sign of the Son of Man will appear in heaven, and then all the tribes of the earth will mourn, and they will see the Son of Man coming on the clouds of heaven with power and great glory."

These passages highlight the significance of celestial signs during the end times as described by Jesus.

The Revelation 12 Sign: A 7-Year Warning to the Church

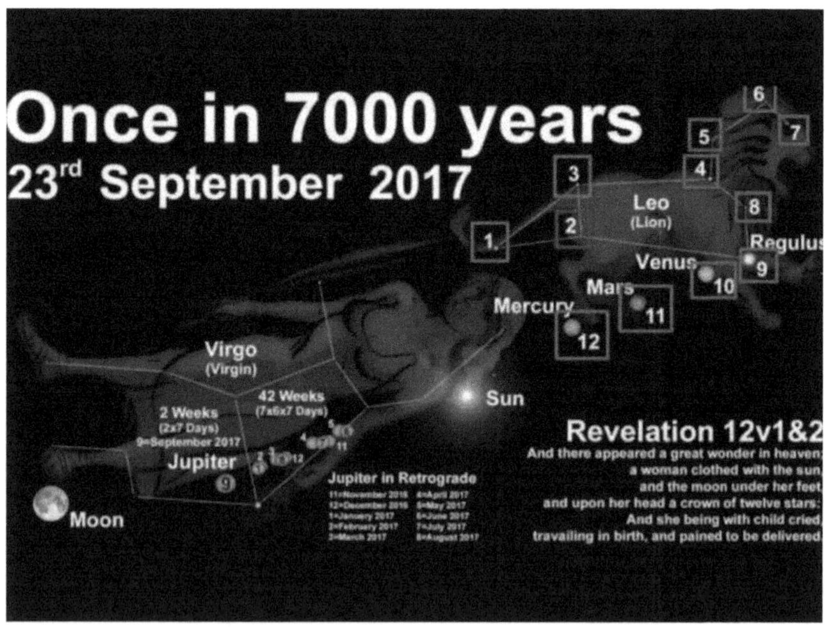

The Revelation 12 sign, as described in the Book of Revelation, has garnered significant attention among Christians, particularly in relation to its prophetic implications for the Church and the end times. This sign, which features a woman clothed with the sun, a dragon, and a male child, is interpreted by many as a powerful symbol of God's divine plan. The seven-year period surrounding this sign, notably from 2017 to 2024, is seen by some believers as a crucial warning that may signal the Rapture sometime around 2024.

In Revelation 12:1-5, the imagery of the woman is often understood to represent Israel, the nation chosen by God to give birth to the Messiah, portrayed as the male child destined to rule all nations. The dragon, identified as Satan, symbolizes the opposition faced by God's purposes throughout history. This narrative encapsulates the ongoing spiritual battle between good and evil, reminding Christians that their faith journey is part of a larger cosmic struggle.

The significance of the Revelation 12 sign is heightened when considering the seven-year timeline that many prophecy scholars link to it. The celestial alignment first observed in September 2017 has been interpreted as the fulfillment of this sign, suggesting that it serves as a warning to the Church about the imminent events leading to the end times.

For Christians, recognizing the Revelation 12 sign as a potential warning emphasizes the urgency for spiritual preparedness. The anticipation of the Rapture calls believers to deepen their faith, engage in prayer, and actively share the message of salvation. Understanding that the events of the next few years could unfold rapidly encourages Christians to live with intention and purpose, focusing on their relationship with God and the mission of spreading the Gospel.

Moreover, the Revelation 12 sign highlights the vital role of Israel in God's prophetic plan. As believers acknowledge Israel's significance in the fulfillment of biblical prophecy, they are called to support and pray for the Jewish people, affirming the belief that God's covenant with Israel remains steadfast.

In conclusion, the Revelation 12 sign serves as a profound warning for the Church, particularly with the possibility that it marks a seven-year countdown leading to the beginning of the tribulation. This sign not only highlights the cosmic struggle between good and evil but also calls Christians to be spiritually prepared for the challenges that lie ahead. The Revelation 12 sign stands as a compelling testament to God's sovereignty and the hope that awaits those who trust in Him during these critical times.

The Prophetic Significance of the Great American Eclipses of 2017 and 2024

The Great American Eclipse of August 21, 2017, and the subsequent solar eclipse on April 8, 2024, have garnered significant attention not only for their astronomical marvels but also for their potential prophetic implications. These events are particularly notable for their paths intersecting towns with names that carry deep biblical significance—seven towns named Salem during the 2017 eclipse and six towns named Nineveh, along with one named Jonah, during the 2024 eclipse. Together, they form an "X" across the United States, leading many to explore their potential messages for the nation and the Church.

The 2017 eclipse, which traveled from coast to coast, passed over seven towns named Salem. The word "Salem" means "peace" in Hebrew and is biblically associated with the city of Jerusalem. The presence of this name in multiple locations along the path of the eclipse invites reflection on themes of peace, restoration, and divine favor. Many Christians viewed this eclipse as a sign from God, interpreting it as an encouragement for the nation to seek peace and reconciliation, both spiritually and socially.

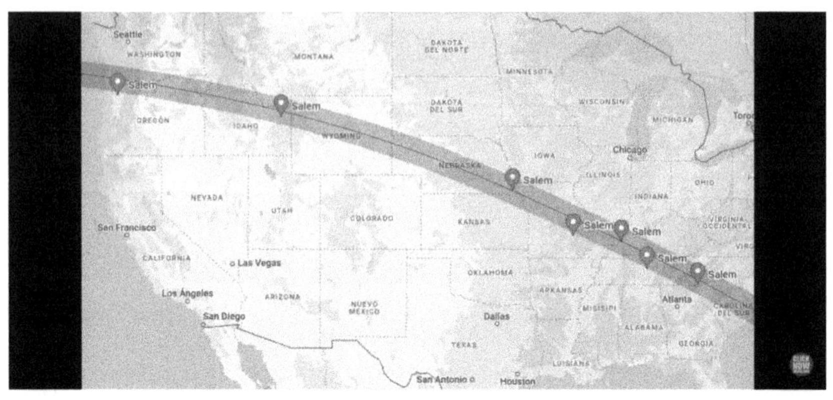

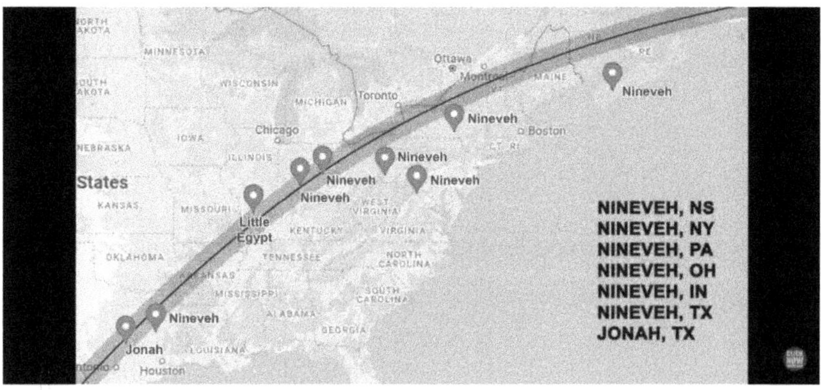

Fast forward to the eclipse on April 8, 2024, which crosses the path of the 2017 eclipse, creating an "X" over the U.S. This eclipse notably passes over six towns named Nineveh and one town called Jonah. Nineveh, known as the capital of the ancient Assyrian Empire, carries a significant biblical narrative, particularly in the Book of Jonah, where God calls Jonah to deliver a message of repentance to its people. The connection between these towns and the themes of repentance, mercy, and divine intervention cannot be overlooked. The "X" formed by these eclipses may symbolize a crossroads for the nation, urging believers to consider their spiritual state and the need for a return to God.

From a prophetic perspective, the alignment of these eclipses over towns...

with such meaningful names may represent a divine warning and a call to action. The seven-year period between the two eclipses could be interpreted as a time of grace and warning, inviting the Church to engage in prayer, repentance,

Explosive 'devil comet' returns for 1st time in 71 years during April 8 eclipse, NASA says

Officially named 12P/Pons-Brooks, the "devil comet" has periodic explosions.

By **Leah Sarnoff** and **Mary Kekatos**
March 18, 2024, 2:00 PM ET • 7 min read

and revival. The eclipses serve as reminders of God's sovereignty and His active role in the affairs of humanity, prompting believers to reflect on their faith and seek a deeper relationship with Him.

Moreover, the significance of these towns—Salem, Nineveh, and Jonah—highlights the importance of responding to God's call. Just as Jonah was sent to Nineveh to proclaim a message of repentance, so too are Christians called to share the Gospel and encourage a return to biblical values in a time when moral and social challenges abound.

In conclusion, the Great American Eclipses of 2017 and 2024, marked by their paths over towns named Salem, Nineveh, and Jonah, hold profound prophetic implications for the United States and the Church. The symbolism of peace, repentance, and divine intervention invites believers to seek God's guidance and to engage actively in the spiritual renewal of the nation.

CHAPTER 8

7000 YEAR SABBATICAL TIMELINE

The 7000-Year Sabbatical Timeline: From the Fall of Adam and Eve to the Millennial Reign of Christ

The concept of a 7000-year timeline, often referred to as the "Sabbatical timeline," is derived from biblical interpretations that link humanity's history to the seven days of creation in Genesis. This framework posits that God's plan for humanity spans seven millennia, with the first six representing periods of human history and the seventh symbolizing the millennial reign of Christ. This chapter explores this timeline, beginning with the sin of Adam and Eve in the Garden of Eden and concluding with the anticipated second coming of Christ and the establishment of His thousand-year reign.

The Beginning: The Fall of Adam and Eve

The timeline commences with the creation of humanity as described in **Genesis 1-2**. Adam and Eve were placed in the Garden of Eden, living in perfect harmony with God. However, their disobedience, as recorded in **Genesis 3**, led to the fall—a pivotal moment that introduced sin into the world. This act of rebellion not only severed the relationship between God and humanity but also set in motion the consequences of sin, including death and separation from God. The fall of Adam and Eve marks the beginning of humanity's struggle and the unfolding of God's redemptive plan.

The First Two Millennia: From Creation to the Flood

Following the fall, the timeline progresses through a period of approximately 2000 years, encompassing significant events in biblical history. This era includes the genealogies from Adam to Noah, highlighting the increasing wickedness of humanity, which culminated in God's decision to cleanse the earth through the Great Flood (**Genesis 6-9**). The flood represents a divine reset, preserving Noah and his family as a remnant to repopulate the earth.

After the flood, humanity began to multiply once again, leading to the Tower of Babel incident (**Genesis 11**), where God confused their languages and scattered them across the earth. This period is often associated with the establishment of nations and cultures, setting the stage for God's covenant with Abraham, which would unfold in the subsequent millennium.

The Second Millennium: The Patriarchs to the Exodus

The second millennium, spanning from approximately 2000 BC to 1000 BC, is characterized by the lives of the patriarchs: Abraham, Isaac, Jacob, and Joseph. God's covenant with Abraham (**Genesis 12**) establishes a chosen people through whom He would reveal Himself to the world. This era continues through the narrative of the Israelites, their enslavement in Egypt, and their eventual deliverance through Moses, culminating in the Exodus (**Exodus 12-14**).

This period also includes the giving of the Law at Mount Sinai (**Exodus 19-20**), which serves as a foundational moment for Israel's identity as God's chosen people. The Israelites' journey to the Promised Land reflects God's faithfulness to His covenant, while their struggles reveal the ongoing tension between divine purpose and human disobedience.

The Third Millennium: The Kingdom and the Prophets

The timeline continues into the third millennium, which encompasses the establishment of the monarchy in Israel, beginning with Saul, followed by David and Solomon. This era (approximately 1000 BC to 0 AD) is marked by the height of Israel's power and prosperity, as well as its eventual decline due to disobedience to God's commandments.

The prophets emerge during this time, calling Israel to repentance and foretelling the coming of the Messiah. Key prophetic texts, such as Isaiah 53, reveal God's plan for redemption through suffering. The prophetic voices serve as reminders of God's commitment to His people and the promise of a future hope.

The Fourth Millennium: The Birth of Christ and the Early Church

The fourth millennium is anchored by the birth of Jesus Christ, marking a significant turning point in human history. The incarnation of Christ (approximately 4 BC) fulfills the messianic prophecies and initiates the New Covenant. Jesus' ministry, death, and resurrection (approximately AD 30) provide the ultimate solution to humanity's sin problem, offering redemption and reconciliation with God.

Following Christ's ascension, the early church is established, empowered by the Holy Spirit at Pentecost (**Acts 2**). The spread of the Gospel throughout the Roman Empire signifies the expansion of God's kingdom and the inclusion of Gentiles into His redemptive plan. This period, often referred to as the Church Age, emphasizes the call for believers to share the message of salvation with the world.

The Fifth to Sixth Millennia: The Present Age and the End Times

As the timeline progresses into the fifth and sixth millennia, scholars often interpret this period as representative of the current age of the church, marked by a mixture of faith and apostasy. This era includes significant events such as the rise of false teachings, moral decline, and the fulfillment of prophetic signs pointing toward the imminent return of Christ.

In **Matthew 24** and **1 Thessalonians 4:16-17**, Jesus' second coming is foretold, emphasizing the need for vigilance and readiness among believers. The concept of a "great falling away" (**2 Thessalonians 2:3**) precedes His return, highlighting the challenges faced by the church in the last days.

The Seventh Millennium: The Millennial Reign of Christ

The culmination of the 7000-year timeline is the establishment of Christ's millennial reign, as described in **Revelation 20:1-6**. This thousand-year period is characterized by peace, justice, and the fulfillment of God's promises to His people. Christ reigns as King, and believers enjoy a restored relationship with God, free from the influence of sin and death.

The millennial kingdom represents the ultimate realization of God's redemptive plan, where His presence dwells among His people. After this period, the final judgment occurs, leading to the new heaven and new earth (**Revelation 21-22**), completing the divine narrative of creation, fall, redemption, and restoration.

Conclusion

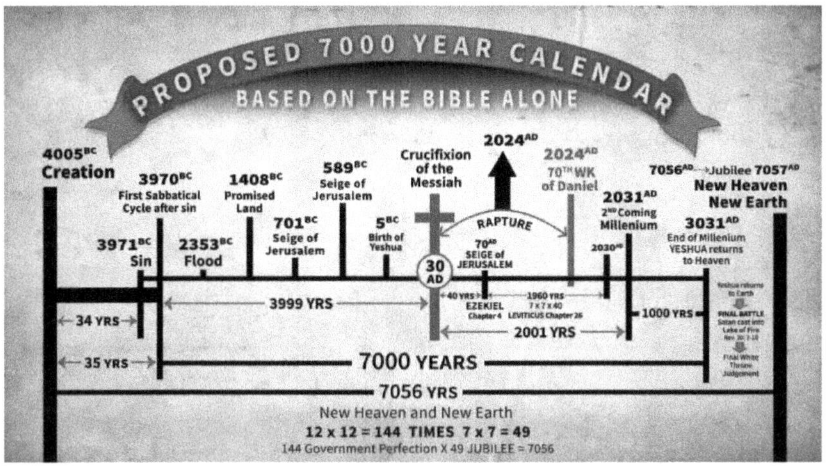

The 7000-year Sabbatical timeline, beginning with the sin of Adam and Eve and culminating in the millennial reign of Christ, reflects the overarching narrative of Scripture. This framework highlights God's sovereignty, faithfulness, and redemptive purpose throughout human history. Each millennium represents critical moments in the unfolding plan of salvation, culminating in the promise of eternal life and restoration for those who believe. As believers await the return of

Christ, the timeline serves as a reminder of the hope and assurance found in God's ultimate plan for humanity.

So, what we are seeing is where we are on God's timetable. The charts created by Rock Island Book Ministries provide a clear picture.

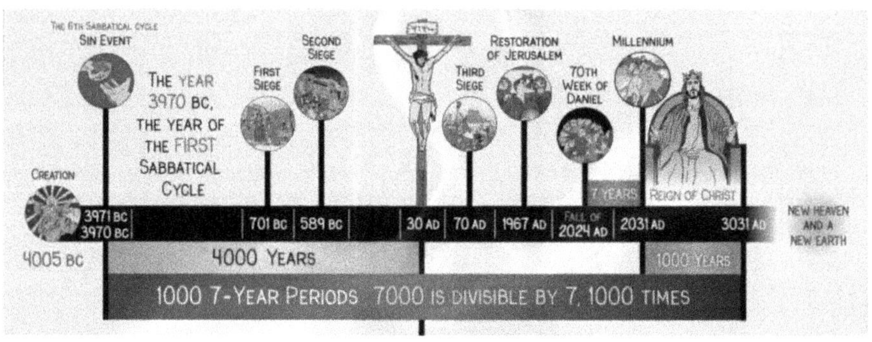

The year 3971 BC is generally considered to be the year that man sinned, which started the clock for God's redemption plan.

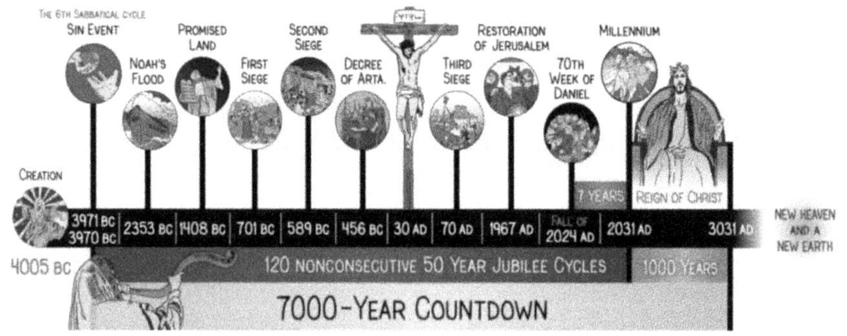

To calculate how many years ago 3971 BC is from the current year (2024 CE), we first calculate from 3971 BC to 1 BC, which is 3970 years (since there is no year 0). Then, from 1 CE to 2024 CE is 2023 years.

Now, add these two amounts together:

3970 years + 2023 years = 5993 years.

Therefore, 3971 BC was 5993 years ago from our current year, 2024.

So, by adding 7 more years to complete 6000 years, we arrive at the year 2031 as the potential return of Jesus Christ to earth to set up His millennial kingdom. If this is the case, then we subtract 7 years for the start of the tribulation, which would place it in the year 2024.

Thus, the next prophecy to be fulfilled is the Rapture of the Church. This event must occur first because the Antichrist will not be revealed until after the Church is gone. Daniel 9:27 speaks of the seven-year peace treaty that the Antichrist brokers with Israel and the rest of the nations, and that peace treaty is what starts the tribulation.

What is obvious now is that there is a gap of time between the Rapture and the start of the tribulation. It's important to understand that it's not the Rapture that kicks off the...

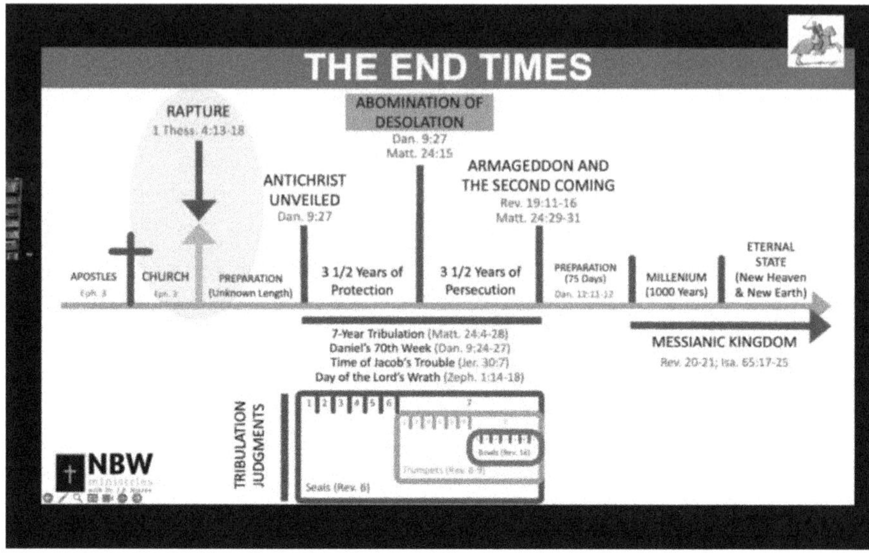

The tribulation is not triggered by the Rapture; it's the signing of the seven-year peace treaty by the Antichrist that marks its beginning. It will take some time for the Antichrist to rise to power once the Church is removed and the Holy Spirit steps aside.

Now, let's explore the gap period between the Rapture and the start of Daniel's 70th week.

In the Book of Daniel, particularly Chapter 11 and in reference to Chapter 8, verse 3 identifies the "little horn" as the Antichrist. Verse 8 discusses historical events surrounding Greece, highlighting its division into four sections, from which the Antichrist is prophesied to emerge. This shift from the historical context in verse 8 to future implications in verse 9 confirms that the Antichrist will arise from one of the four divisions of the Greek Empire.

As we delve deeper into Daniel Chapter 11, the text clarifies the specific division that will give rise to the Antichrist. The chapter begins by outlining the historical backdrop of Greece and Persia, emphasizing Greece's fragmentation into four kingdoms—a concept introduced in Chapter 8. Verse 4 refers to these four kingdoms, linking them to the imagery of the two legs in Daniel Chapter 2, verse 5.

Verse 5 shifts focus to the "king of the south," who will possess significant strength, alongside one of his princes who will rise above him, establishing a considerable dominion. Transitioning from verse 5 to verse 6 marks a movement from historical references to future prophetic events. Many biblical scholars, including Schofield, Larkin, and Trevor, categorize verses 5 through 21 as historical, concluding with the appearance of the Antichrist in verse 21. However, many watchmen today contend that the events between verses 6 and 21 are prophetic occurrences that will unfold after the Rapture and before the seven-year peace agreement, signaling the start of the 70th week.

This prophetic timeline indicates that three kings from the north will be addressed. It is evident that there exists a gap in the timeline of prophecy, which is elaborated upon throughout the Book of Daniel. These events will occur after the conclusion of the dispensation of grace, which currently prevents these prophecies from manifesting. Consequently, there will be a distinct interval following the Rapture and preceding the commencement of the seventh week, during which significant prophetic events will unfold. Many believe that we are nearing a crucial moment, with 2031 potentially marking the second coming of the Lord to establish His millennial kingdom. The unfolding events around us serve as indicators of this imminent reality.

My exploration of Bible prophecy began at the age of 15, focused on the anticipation of the Rapture. At this juncture, it feels akin to the final stages of a treasure hunt. Initially, we explored the entire world, identifying the correct continent, country, province, state, and now, the specific town. We have pinpointed the precise location where the treasure—the Rapture and resurrection—is imminently close.

Currently, we find ourselves meticulously examining every sign. Rather than making broad projections, we are honing in on shorter intervals and specific details. After years of making significant predictions, it is evident that we are now in the final countdown. As we are in the year 2024, if Christ returns for His Church, we will have seven years to fulfill what is prophesied. According to Daniel 9:27, the Antichrist will establish a seven-year covenant, but a crucial variable arises. In Matthew 24:22, Jesus states that those days will be shortened for the sake of the elect, introducing uncertainty regarding the duration of the seven years—whether it may start late or conclude early.

Revelation 12:12 reveals that Satan is filled with wrath because he knows his time is short. This verse encourages the heavens to rejoice, as the Church will have been raptured before the tribulation commences. Those left behind—referred to as the inhabitants of the earth and the sea—will face the consequences of this wrath as the devil is cast down to them. This casting down signifies a specific and brief period right before Christ's second coming, during which the devil is confined to Earth.

Satan's awareness of this limited timeframe implies that he knows the tribulation may be shortened. Had the tribulation begun on time, he would not anticipate its early conclusion. His meticulously calculated plan over the past 2,000 years is now threatened. He expected seven full years to execute his strategies, but with the divine shortening of this period, he is left scrambling.

Considering how these days may be shortened, adjustments could occur both at the beginning and the end of the tribulation. For instance, if the Rapture were to happen at the Feast of Trumpets this October, and the tribulation were to commence in the fall of 2025, this would give the Antichrist a year to rise to power while the world transitions to a new system. This scenario would shorten the tribulation from seven to six years, still aligning with God's 7,000-year sabbatical calendar. Current events may reflect the beginnings of conflicts described in Psalm 83 and Jeremiah 49, potentially leading to the destruction of Damascus as stated in Isaiah 17, which could precede the Gog and Magog war in Ezekiel 38 and 39.

As watchmen, we continually adapt our understanding and interpretations. Over the past 40 years, I have sought signs, and since 2020, particularly with the onset of COVID-19, I have intensified my studies. The rapidity with which signs are diminishing is striking and serves as a clear indicator of how close we are to significant events.

This understanding prompts profound personal reflection on my life, spiritual practices, and the company I keep. It underscores the urgency of maintaining a strong prayer life and a deep commitment to Scripture. What a remarkable time to be alive! The prospect of experiencing the presence of Jesus is exhilarating, and I can only imagine the joy and awe that will accompany that moment.

The seven-year tribulation is a significant period in biblical prophecy, primarily described in the Book of Revelation and the prophetic writings of Daniel. This time is characterized by intense suffering, trials, and the final confrontation between good and evil. In the next chapter, we'll provide an explanation of the events that are believed to unfold during this tumultuous period.

CHAPTER 9

7 YEAR TRIBULATION

Introduction to the Tribulation

Without going into great detail, since we—the Church—won't be here for the tribulation, this chapter will give a general outline of the events described in Revelation. The tribulation is divided into two halves: the first three and a half years, known as the "beginning of sorrows," and the second half, referred to as the "Great Tribulation." This period is precipitated by the Rapture of the Church, where believers are taken up to meet Christ, leaving the world to face the ensuing judgments.

The Rise of the Antichrist

At the start of the tribulation, a charismatic leader known as the Antichrist will emerge. He will gain power and influence, initially presenting himself as a man of peace. The Antichrist will establish a global government and a false sense of security, eventually making a covenant with Israel for seven years, which will be broken halfway through the tribulation.

The Seals (Revelation 6-7)

The tribulation begins with the opening of the seven seals by Jesus, the Lamb of God:

1. First Seal: A rider on a white horse, representing conquest and the Antichrist's rise to power.

2. Second Seal: A rider on a red horse, symbolizing war and bloodshed.

3. Third Seal: A rider on a black horse, representing famine and economic distress.

4. Fourth Seal: A rider on a pale horse, representing death and Hades, indicating widespread mortality.

5. Fifth Seal: The souls of martyrs cry out for justice, indicating persecution against believers.

6. Sixth Seal: Cosmic disturbances, including earthquakes, eclipses, and a great shaking of the heavens.

The Trumpets (Revelation 8-9)

Following the seals, seven trumpets are sounded, each heralding further judgments:

1. First Trumpet: Hail and fire mixed with blood, destroying a third of the earth's vegetation.

2. Second Trumpet: A great mountain burning with fire is thrown into the sea, killing a third of marine life.

3. Third Trumpet: A star named Wormwood falls, poisoning a third of the waters.

4. Fourth Trumpet: A third of the sun, moon, and stars are darkened.

5. Fifth Trumpet: The opening of the Abyss, unleashing locust-like creatures to torment those without the seal of God.

6. Sixth Trumpet: A massive army is unleashed, resulting in the death of a third of mankind.

The Bowl Judgments (Revelation 16)

The final series of judgments are the seven bowl judgments, which are more severe and direct during the Great Tribulation:

1. First Bowl: Sores break out on those who have the mark of the beast.

2. Second Bowl: The sea turns to blood, killing all marine life.

3. Third Bowl: The rivers and springs become blood.

4. Fourth Bowl: Scorching heat from the sun.

5. Fifth Bowl: Darkness and pain in the kingdom of the beast.

6. Sixth Bowl: The Euphrates River dries up, preparing the way
    for the kings of the East and the battle of Armageddon.

7. Seventh Bowl: A loud voice declares, "It is done!" and the
    greatest earthquake occurs, resulting in the destruction of
    cities and islands.

The Great Tribulation

The second half of the tribulation is marked by unprecedented
suffering and the wrath of God. During this time, the Antichrist will
demand worship, instituting the mark of the beast (Revelation 13:16-
18), which will be required for buying and selling. Those who refuse to
take the mark will face persecution and death.

The Battle of Armageddon

As the tribulation reaches its climax, the armies of the world will gather
in the Valley of Megiddo for the final confrontation against God's
people. This battle, known as Armageddon, will culminate in Christ's
return to defeat the Antichrist and his forces.

The Second Coming of Christ

At the conclusion of the tribulation, Jesus Christ will return in glory to establish His kingdom on earth. This event, known as the Second Coming, will be visible to all, and He will destroy the Antichrist and the false prophet, casting them into the lake of fire.

The Establishment of Christ's Millennial Reign

Following the tribulation, Christ will establish a 1,000-year reign known as the Millennium, during which peace and righteousness will prevail. This period will fulfill many of God's promises to Israel and allow for a time of restoration and blessing.

Conclusion

The seven-year tribulation is a time of severe judgment and testing for humanity, serving as a backdrop for the ultimate triumph of God's kingdom.

CHAPTER 10

THE 7 FEASTS OF ISRAEL

The Seven Feasts of Israel: Their Significance and Connection to the First and Second Coming of Christ

The seven feasts of Israel, as outlined in the Torah and the Bible (specifically in Leviticus 23), are crucial elements of Jewish identity and worship. Each feast holds deep spiritual significance and prophetic implications, particularly concerning the first and second comings of Jesus Christ. This chapter explores these feasts, their meanings, and how they relate to the life and ministry of Jesus.

THE SEVEN JEWISH FEASTS

Appointed Feasts and Holy Convocations of Leviticus 23

"These are a shadow of the things that were to come; the reality, however, is found in Christ"
Colossians 2:17

Passover (Pesach)

1. Biblical Significance: Passover commemorates the Israelites' deliverance from slavery in Egypt. It involves the sacrifice of a lamb, whose blood was smeared on the doorposts to protect the inhabitants from the final plague—the death of the firstborn.

2. Connection to Christ: Jesus is referred to as the "Lamb of God" in the New Testament (John 1:29). His crucifixion occurred during Passover, symbolizing the ultimate sacrifice for humanity's sins. Just as the blood of the lamb saved the Israelites, Christ's blood redeems believers from spiritual death.

Unleavened Bread (Matzot)

1. Biblical Significance: This feast begins immediately after Passover and lasts for seven days. It symbolizes the haste with which the Israelites left Egypt, without time for their bread to rise.

2. Connection to Christ: Jesus' burial took place during this feast. Leaven often symbolizes sin in the Bible, and Christ, being sinless, represents the "unleavened" bread. His body, laid in the

tomb, signifies the removal of sin for those who believe in Him.

Firstfruits (Bikkurim)

1. Biblical Significance: This feast celebrates the beginning of the harvest. Israelites would bring the first sheaf of barley to the temple as an offering to God.

2. Connection to Christ: Jesus rose from the dead on the feast of Firstfruits (1 Corinthians 15:20), making Him the "firstfruits" of those who have died. His resurrection assures believers of their future resurrection, marking the start of God's harvest of souls.

Pentecost (Shavuot)

1. Biblical Significance: Celebrated fifty days after First fruits, Pentecost marks the end of the grain harvest and commemorates the giving of the Torah at Mount Sinai.

2. Connection to Christ: Pentecost is significant in the New Testament as the day the Holy Spirit descended upon the apostles (Acts 2). This event empowered them to spread the

gospel, establishing the Church. The giving of the Holy Spirit fulfills Jesus' promise of a Comforter after His earthly ministry.

Feast of Trumpets (Rosh Hashanah)

1. Biblical Significance: This feast marks the Jewish New Year and is a time of reflection, repentance, and preparation for the Day of Atonement. The sounding of the shofar (trumpet) calls people to gather and prepare for the upcoming solemn days.

2. Connection to Christ: This feast is closely associated with the Rapture of the Church, symbolizing the divine call for God's people. The Apostle Paul emphasizes this connection in scripture, stating that the Lord will descend with a shout accompanied by the trumpet of God (1 Thessalonians 4:16). He further elaborates that "in a moment, in the twinkling of an eye, at the last trumpet, the trumpet will sound, and the dead will be raised imperishable, and we shall be changed" (1 Corinthians 15:51–52). This heralds the resurrection of those who have died in Christ and the eventual gathering of believers.

Day of Atonement (Yom Kippur)

1. Biblical Significance: This is the holiest day in the Jewish calendar, dedicated to atonement and repentance. It involves fasting and the ceremonial casting away of sins onto a scapegoat.

2. Connection to Christ: Jesus' sacrificial death serves as the ultimate fulfillment of the Day of Atonement. He is the scapegoat who bears the sins of humanity (Isaiah 53:6). His atoning sacrifice reconciles believers to God, providing the means for eternal life. The future fulfillment of this feast is seen in the promise of Christ's return to earth to judge the living and the dead.

Tabernacles (Sukkot)

1. Biblical Significance: This feast celebrates the harvest and commemorates the Israelites' forty years of wandering in the wilderness, living in temporary shelters (sukkot).

2. Connection to Christ: Jesus' incarnation during the Feast of Tabernacles is significant; He "tabernacled"

among us (John 1:14). The future fulfillment of this feast is seen in the promise of Christ's 1,000-year reign, where He will dwell among His people and then create the new heaven and new earth (Revelation 21:3).

Conclusion

The seven feasts of Israel are rich in spiritual significance and prophetic meaning. They not only commemorate key historical events in Jewish history but also foreshadow the redemptive work of Jesus Christ in His first coming and the promises associated with His second coming. By understanding these feasts, believers gain deeper insight into the continuity of God's plan for humanity and the fulfillment of His promises through Christ. Each feast serves as a prophetic timeline. Since the spring feasts have already been fulfilled to the day, we are anticipating the fall feasts to also be fulfilled to the day.

The next feast to be fulfilled is the Feast of Trumpets, which is observed on the first day of the month of Tishrei, typically falling in September or October. This year, in 2024, it falls on October 2nd and 3rd, coinciding with a solar eclipse, which is generally associated with the Church, as opposed to blood moons, which are associated with Israel. This feast is rooted in biblical scripture, specifically in Leviticus 23:23-

25, where God commands the Israelites to observe a day of rest marked by the blowing of trumpets:

"In a moment, in the twinkling of an eye, at the last trumpet. For the trumpet will sound, and the dead will be raised imperishable, and we shall be changed." (1 Corinthians 15:51–52)

Ancient Jews relied on a calendar based on actual cycles of the moon, not one arbitrarily set. Thus, the key to determining the first day of each month was the sighting of the new moon. It was so important that it required confirmation by two or more witnesses. Because of difficulties in determining the new moon (it could be obscured by clouds, etc.) and the slowness with which news once traveled, Jewish leaders living outside Israel decided Rosh Hashanah would be celebrated over two days to ensure it was celebrated on the appropriate day. Jewish leaders inside Israel had less difficulty determining the start of the holiday – but still celebrate it over two days for consistency. It is therefore also known as the day no one knows.

Jesus told us in Matthew 24:36: "But concerning that day and hour, no one knows, not even the angels of heaven, nor the Son, but the Father only." He literally did not say year or season.

In 1 Thessalonians 5:1-2, the Apostle Paul speaks to the believers in Thessalonica about the return of Christ, affirming their awareness of the events surrounding it. He emphasizes that there is no need for further instruction on the matter, as they are already aware that the day of the Lord will arrive unexpectedly, akin to a thief in the night.

Similarly, in the Gospel of Matthew, Jesus chastised the Pharisees for their failure to recognize the signs of His coming. In Matthew 16:1-4, when the Pharisees and Sadducees request a heavenly sign, He responds: "An evil and adulterous generation seeks for a sign, but no sign will be given to it except the sign of Jonah." Following this, He departs from them. This response highlights their spiritual blindness and inability to perceive the prophetic fulfillment and the significance of His ministry. The "sign of Jonah" alludes to His death and resurrection, which serve as the definitive affirmation of His authority and messianic identity. Consequently, it is reasonable to assert that the final generation would be informed of the signs marking His imminent return. Furthermore, we are uniquely positioned as the generation capable of understanding the timing of the Lord's return, as indicated in Daniel 12:4, which states: "But you, Daniel, shut up the words and seal the book until the time of the end. Many shall run to and from, and knowledge shall increase." This instruction to seal the prophetic revelations suggests that their complete comprehension would be reserved for a later period, encapsulating the theme of prophecy and the unfolding of God's divine plan during the end times.

CHAPTER 11

THE COMING WARS

"Surely, the Sovereign LORD does nothing without revealing His plan to His servants, the prophets." (Amos 3:7)

Experts in eschatology frequently discuss the Gog-Magog war as foretold in Ezekiel 38-39, a prophecy that suggests a formidable alliance, likely spearheaded by Russia, will one day invade Israel. Some speculate that the fulfillment of this prophecy may be imminent.

Ezekiel 38:1-6 NIV

The word of the LORD came to me:

"Son of man, set your face against Gog, of the land of Magog, the chief prince of Meshek and Tubal; prophesy against him and say: 'This is what the Sovereign Lord says: I am against you, Gog, chief prince of Meshek and Tubal. I will turn you around, put hooks in your jaws and bring you out with your whole army—your horses, your horsemen fully armed, and a great horde with large and small shields, all of them brandishing their swords. Persia, Cush and Put will be with them, all with shields and helmets, also Gomer with all its troops, and Beth

Togarmah from the far north with all its troops—the many nations with you...'"

However, a lesser-known prophecy is gaining significance in contemporary discourse: Psalm 83. This psalm describes a confederation that seeks the annihilation of Israel, reflecting the ongoing war and tensions in the Middle East where nations conspire to eliminate the Jewish state.

And faithfulness of God in keeping His promises," Asaph implies through his psalm. The prophetic text lists the members of this coalition:

1. Edomites: Modern-day southern Jordan, closely related to Israel through Esau, Jacob's brother.

2. Ishmaelites: Descendants of Ishmael, traditionally associated with Arab nations.

3. Moabites: Present-day central Jordan, originating from Lot's elder daughter.

4. Hagrites: An obscure group, potentially linked to nomadic tribes in the Arabian Desert.

5. Gebalites: Believed to inhabit present-day Lebanon.

6. Ammonites: Located in modern-day northern Jordan, also descendants of Lot.

7. Amalekites: A nomadic tribe with historical enmity towards Israel, possibly from the Sinai Peninsula region.

8. Philistines: Ancient inhabitants of the Gaza region, whose legacy persists in the name "Palestine."

9. Tyre: A city in modern-day Lebanon, known for its historical Phoenician influence.

10. Assyrians: An empire based in present-day northern Iraq and parts of Syria.

The Psalm 83 coalition represents nations surrounding Israel, many of which share a deep-seated historical and ideological opposition to the Jewish state.

Implications for Modern Times

As the Middle East remains a hotspot for conflict, with various coalitions forming and dissolving over shared interests, the alignment of nations mentioned in Psalm 83 with modern entities has not gone unnoticed by scholars of prophecy. These scholars often draw parallels between the ancient tribes and contemporary nations or groups, seeing the continued tension in the region as a possible precursor to the fulfillment of Asaph's prophecy.

The Connection with the Gog-Magog Prophecy

While the Gog-Magog war described in Ezekiel 38-39 involves a larger, possibly global alliance against Israel led by a distant power (often interpreted as Russia), the Psalm 83 conflict appears to involve Israel's immediate neighbors. Some eschatologists argue that the Psalm 83 war could precede the Gog-Magog battle, weakening Israel's neighbors and setting the stage for the larger global confrontation.

Concluding Thoughts

The study of Psalm 83 offers a compelling perspective on the current geopolitical climate in the Middle East. As nations continue to vie for power and influence in the region, the ancient words of Asaph resonate with modern implications. Whether seen as a precursor to the end times or a distinct prophecy yet to be fulfilled, Psalm 83 remains a significant component of eschatological study, reminding believers of the enduring relevance of biblical prophecy in understanding the events of today.

Invader	Location
Edom	Southwest Jordan
Ishmaelites	Arabia
Moab	Central West Jordan
Hagarenes	Sinai
Gebal	Northern Lebanon
Ammon	Northern Jordan
Amalek	Southern Israel or Northern Sinai
Philistia	Southwest Palestine
Tyre	Southwest Lebanon
Assyria	Syria & Northern Iraq
Children of Lot	Moab & Ammon

This section of Psalm 83 highlights the deep-rooted animosity and united intent of these ten groups to erase Israel from the map, reflecting the ongoing spiritual and physical battle over the land promised to the descendants of Abraham, Isaac, and Jacob.

The Ten-Nation Coalition: Modern-Day Implications

1. Edom: Traditionally associated with southern Jordan, Edom's ancient enmity towards Israel symbolizes ongoing regional hostilities.

2. Ishmaelites: Representing Arab nations descending from Ishmael, this group is symbolic of the broader Arab world's historical conflicts with Israel.

3. Moab: Now part of central Jordan, Moab's ancient struggles with Israel echo in current geopolitical tensions.

4. Hagrites: While their exact modern equivalent is uncertain, they likely represent nomadic tribes from the Arabian Peninsula, symbolizing ongoing tribal conflicts and opposition to Israel.

5. Gebal (Byblos): Located in modern-day Lebanon, Gebal's inclusion points to the historical and ongoing tensions between Israel and Lebanon.

6. Ammon: Also linked to modern-day Jordan, Ammon's past enmity with Israel is reflective of some of the strained relations in the region today.

7. Amalek: Often representing the epitome of opposition to Israel, Amalek's legacy continues through any force that seeks Israel's destruction.

8. Philistia: Corresponding to the region of Gaza, this group is historically linked to the Palestinians and represents ongoing conflicts in that area.

9. Tyre: Situated in Lebanon, Tyre's inclusion underscores Lebanon's complex and often adversarial relationship with Israel.

10. Assyria: Representing a vast ancient empire, modern-day counterparts could include parts of Iraq and Syria, nations with a history of opposition to Israel.

The Spiritual Significance

This coalition's efforts to destroy Israel are more than just a political or military alliance; they are seen as an attempt to invalidate God's promises and challenge His sovereignty. The Abrahamic Covenant, the Davidic Covenant, and the New Covenant are all intertwined with Israel's existence and future. Therefore, the annihilation of Israel would represent an assault on the credibility and authority of God's Word.

God's Unfailing Covenant

Despite the threats posed by this coalition, the Bible assures us that God's promises are irrevocable. His covenant with Abraham is described as everlasting, and His commitment to Israel's restoration is unconditional. This divine assurance is not just for Israel's sake but for the sanctity and honor of God's holy name:

1. The Abrahamic Covenant: This foundational promise guarantees the land of Israel to Abraham's descendants forever (Genesis 12:1-3; Genesis 15:18-21).

2. The Davidic Covenant: This covenant promises that David's lineage will continue forever, culminating in the Messiah's eternal reign (2 Samuel 7:12-13; Isaiah 9:6-7).

3. The New Covenant: This ensures an eternal, restored relationship between God and Israel, where He will place His law in their hearts (Jeremiah 31:33).

Conclusion

The prophecy of Psalm 83 is a stark reminder of the ongoing spiritual warfare surrounding Israel. The ten-nation coalition's intent to destroy Israel is not just a physical threat but a spiritual challenge to God's eternal promises. However, Scripture assures us that God's Word is unbreakable, and His covenant with Israel will stand firm against any opposition. The significance of Psalm 83 in eschatology lies in its vivid portrayal of the spiritual and physical battles that have and will continue to define Israel's history and future.

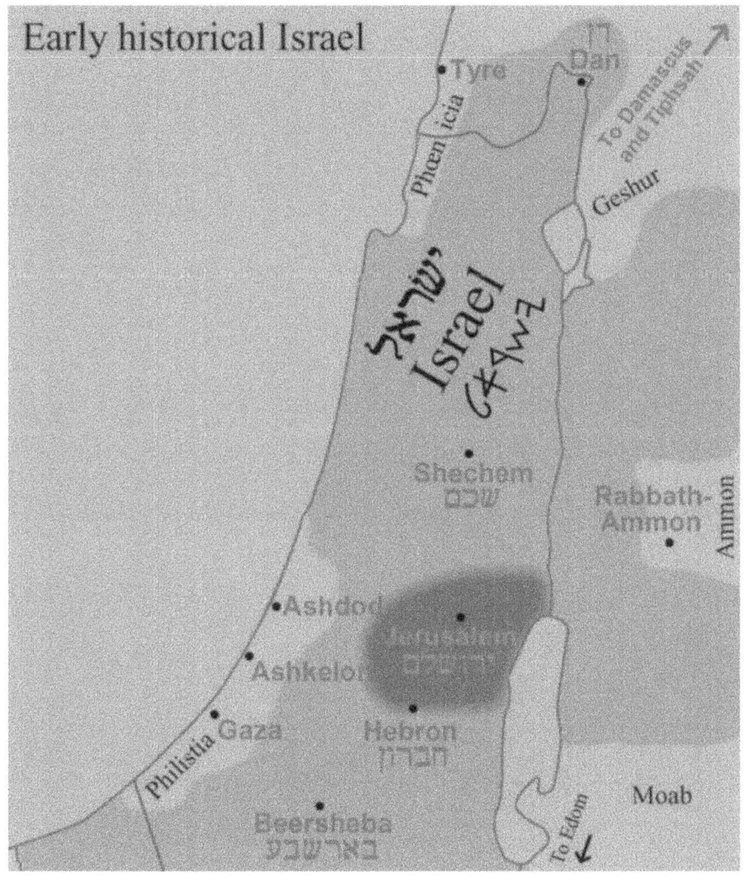

Though these groups may no longer be recognized by their ancient names, modern interpretations suggest their contemporary equivalents:

1. Tents of Edom: Palestinians and Southern Jordanians

2. Ishmaelites: Saudis

3. Moab: Palestinians and Central Jordanians

4. Hagrites: Egyptians

5. Gebal (Byblos): Hezbollah and Northern Lebanese

6. Ammon: Palestinians and Northern Jordanians

7. Amalek: Arabs of the Sinai

8. Philistia: Hamas

9. Tyre: Hezbollah and Southern Lebanese

10. Assyria: Syrians and Northern Iraqis

This coalition, while not overtly united in action against Israel, is inherently aligned under a common Islamic ethos, driven by historical rivalries that date back to Ishmael and Isaac, and Esau and Jacob.

Current Conspiracies and Aspirations

The nations mentioned in Psalm 83 actively seek to undermine Israel's existence, aspiring to transform it into a state incapable of safeguarding its Jewish citizens.

1. Palestinians—Tents of Edom; Moab and Ammon: Mahmoud Abbas, president of the Palestinian Authority, has publicly rejected Israel's identity as a Jewish state, asserting a commitment to march to Jerusalem in defiance.

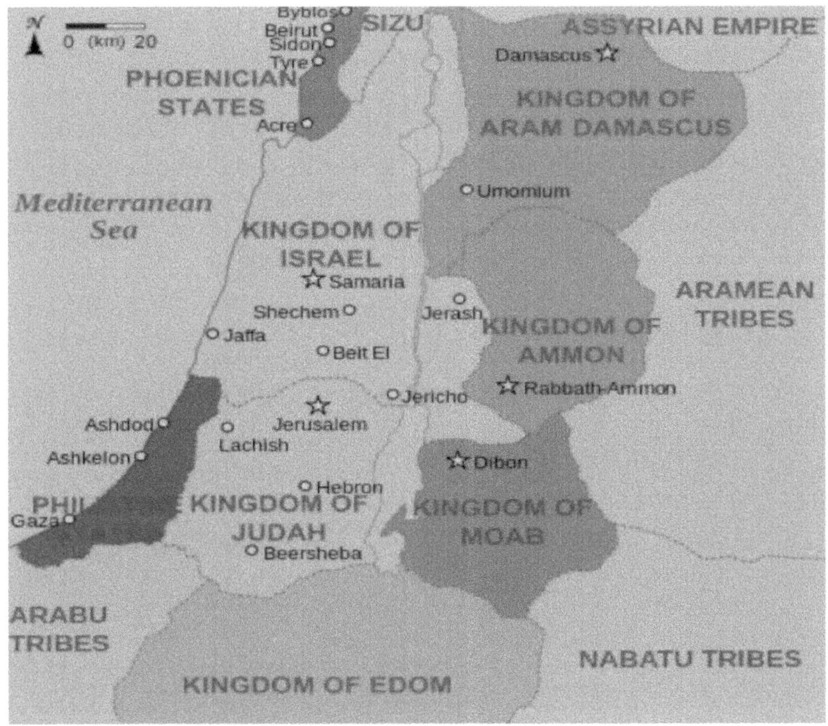

2. Jordanians—Tents of Edom; Moab and Ammon: Despite a longstanding peace treaty with Israel, sentiments against recognizing Israel as a Jewish state persist among Jordanian leaders and the populace.

3. Hezbollah and Lebanon—Gebal (Byblos) and Tyre: Hezbollah's leadership has expressed that the elimination of Israel is paramount to regional interests.

4. Hamas—Philistines: The terrorist organization openly advocates for Israel's destruction, stating unequivocal intentions to resist any semblance of peace.

5. Egyptians (or Northern Jordanians)—Hagrites: While Egypt and Israel have enjoyed a level of cooperation, internal dynamics and historical animosities remain.

6. Saudis (or all Arabs)—Ishmaelites: Saudi Arabia, despite its alliance with the U.S., has historically opposed the establishment of a Jewish state.

7. Arabs of the Sinai—Amalek: This group may represent a segment within Israel that seeks to destabilize the Jewish state.

8. Syrians and Northern Iraqis—Assyria: The absence of diplomatic relations with Syria underscores ongoing hostilities towards Israel.

The Prophet's Appeal for Divine Intervention

In Psalm 83, Asaph implores God to bring disgrace upon the coalition members (Psalm 83:9-18), a theme echoed in other prophetic texts. The expectation of Israel's victory may pave the way for future conflicts, such as the Gog-Magog war outlined in Ezekiel 38—where invaders will seek to exploit Israel's perceived vulnerabilities.

Psalm 83: An Unfulfilled Prophecy

While some theologians assert that the events of Israel's 1948 War for Independence or the 1967 Six-Day War fulfilled Psalm 83, the specific coalition of ten nations identified remains unfulfilled, suggesting that a future conflict will indeed materialize. Jeremiah 49 encompasses prophetic declarations concerning the destinies of various nations, including Elam, which corresponds to present-day Iran. It is believed that Israel may target the nuclear reactor at the Bushehr site in Elam/Iran, leading to the dispersion of its inhabitants, rendering the region uninhabitable.

Context of Judgment

The chapter outlines God's judgment against nations, notably Elam, highlighting themes of destruction and displacement. The prophecy foretells calamity for Elam and the scattering of its population, reflecting a broader divine principle regarding judgment against nations that defy God's will or pose threats to His people.

Symbolism of Destruction

The imagery employed in Jeremiah 49—such as the breaking of Elam's bow and the scattering of its people—can be interpreted symbolically. The bow may represent military power, potentially encompassing modern military threats like nuclear capabilities. This prophecy suggests divine intervention to diminish or eliminate such threats directed at Israel.

Historical and Future Fulfillment

Although the text primarily addresses historical judgments, many interpretations extend to future scenarios. The concept of divine intervention in response to existential threats to Israel aligns with the belief that God safeguards His people and will act against adversaries.

Modern Applications

Contemporary scholars and theologians often connect these prophecies to current geopolitical dynamics, particularly concerning Iran's nuclear ambitions and the possibility of Israeli military action. They may contend that the principles articulated in Jeremiah 49 anticipate a future where Israel takes decisive action to mitigate threats from Iran, illustrating God's continued sovereignty and protective hand over His people.

Summary of These Events

Israel was reestablished as a nation in 1948, fulfilling the prophecy outlined in Ezekiel 36:24. Subsequently, during the remarkable Six-Day War of 1967, Israel regained control over Jerusalem. For end-times prophecies to manifest, it was crucial not only for Israel to exist as a nation but also to hold authority over old Jerusalem and the Temple Mount (see Matthew 24:15-21; Revelation 11:1-2; 2 Thessalonians 2:4).

Additionally, the Gog/Magog prophecy in Ezekiel 38-39 states that Israel's adversaries will perish on the "mountains of Israel," a prophecy that became viable only after the Six-Day War, as prior to that, most of these mountains were under Jordanian control (Ezekiel 39:2).

Israel is anticipated to encounter increasing opposition from neighboring countries, indicating that she will not be living in peace or security. The current Israel-Hamas conflict should not be conflated with the Gog/Magog War. The extensive Gaza-Israel barrier, which took over three years to construct and measures 40 miles long and 20 feet high, was breached by Hamas, demonstrating that Israel was not secure when the attacks began on October 7 of this year.

As Israel faces a coalition of ten nations in what is termed the Psalm 83 War (Psalm 83:2-8), it is evident that Israel will triumph over these foes, surprising the international community. This victory is significant as it sets the stage for Israel to be living securely before the subsequent Gog/Magog conflict. The complete destruction of Damascus is prophesied (Isaiah 17:1), likely by nuclear weapons, although the timeline remains uncertain; it may align with the Psalm 83 War, supported by the description in Jeremiah 49:24, which depicts Damascus in turmoil. Moreover, Jesus referred to the events preceding the Tribulation as "the beginning of birth pains" (Matthew 24:8), adding another layer to this interpretation.

The current conflict may signify the onset of the Psalm 83 War, especially since none of Israel's neighboring states mentioned in Psalm 83:6-8 are included among the invading forces in the Gog/Magog War, suggesting they have been subdued.

Following this victory, there is speculation that Israel may expand its territory, as suggested by pastor and author Bill Salus and others. While it is possible that Israel could exert control over these nations as territories, it is not believed that the Psalm 83 War will lead to the annihilation of Israel's neighbors; rather, it will subdue them, rendering them incapable of posing a threat. This belief is rooted in the scriptural understanding that Jesus Christ will ultimately judge some of these nations upon His return.

The construction of the Third Temple in Jerusalem is a certainty, though its timing remains uncertain (Matthew 24:15-21; Revelation 11:1-2; 2 Thessalonians 2:4). It is plausible that the Temple could be rebuilt during a brief period of security following the Psalm 83 War and preceding the Gog/Magog War, especially as preparations for its construction are already in place.

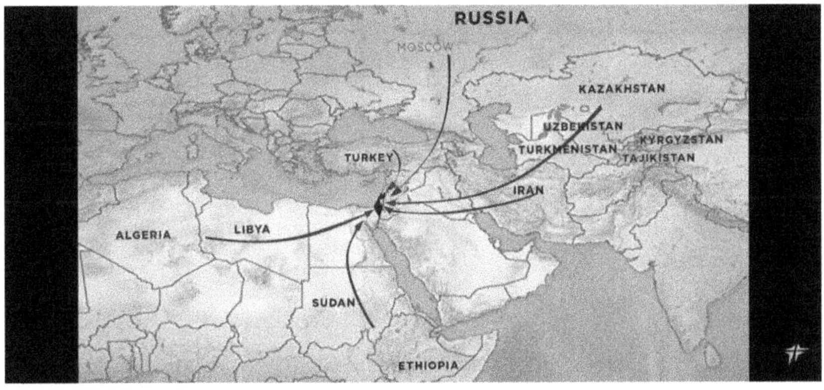

As the Gog/Magog War commences, Iran is likely to react vehemently to the outcomes of the Psalm 83 War, having financially supported many of the groups Israel has just defeated, including Hezbollah, Hamas, and various Shi'ite militias. In retaliation, Iran will incite the Gog/Magog War in alliance with nations such as Russia, Turkey, and others (Ezekiel 38-39). God will instigate a movement against Israel, described as a land restored from war and populated from various nations (Ezekiel 38:8). The invaders will devise a scheme to attack the land of unwalled villages, believing they can overtake a people living in false security (Ezekiel 38:10-11).

God Himself will intervene decisively, defeating this coalition and astonishing the world, thereby bringing glory to His name (Ezekiel 38:18-23; 39:1-13). The invading forces will be vanquished through divine intervention utilizing various means of destruction, including earthquakes, confusion, pestilence, and catastrophic weather phenomena (Ezekiel 38:19-22). Through these events, God will sanctify His name before both Jews and Gentiles (Ezekiel 38:23; 39:7).

The Church may experience the Rapture during this time, though it could occur slightly earlier or later (1 Thessalonians 4:13-18; Revelation 4:1).

Following Israel's miraculous victory, the Antichrist will approach the nation, promising peace and protection for seven years. Despite having rejected Jesus, Israel will accept the Antichrist, in line with Jesus' prophecy (John 5:43). This acceptance will initiate the Tribulation, described as a "time of distress for Jacob" (Daniel 9:27; Jeremiah 30:7).

Midway through the seven-year Tribulation period, the Antichrist will be killed and resurrected, leading the astonished inhabitants of the earth to worship him (Revelation 13:3-4). In a rage of self-obsession, he will establish his throne in the Temple of God in Jerusalem, declaring himself to be God (Matthew 24:15-21; 2 Thessalonians 2:3-4). Through the False Prophet, he will demand global worship, enforcing the acceptance of his mark, which will lead to eternal condemnation for unbelievers (Revelation 13:8, 12, 14-17; 14:9-11; 16:2; 19:20; 20:4).

Jesus will return to defeat the Antichrist and his forces in the Battle of Armageddon, the final confrontation on earth (Psalm 2; 2 Thessalonians 2:8; Revelation 16:12-16).

The inhabitants of the earth will face judgment before the Lord Jesus in two distinct judgments: one for Gentiles (Joel 3:1-3; Matthew 25:31-46) and one for Israel (Ezekiel 20:35-38). Those deemed worthy will enter the Millennial Kingdom, while the others will be confined to a place of torment until the Great White Throne judgment.

The Millennial reign of Christ will commence, with Jesus ruling from Mt. Zion, the highest point on earth at that time (Psalm 48:1; Isaiah 2:2-4; Revelation 20:1-6).

At the conclusion of the Kingdom Age, Satan will be released briefly, inciting rebellion against Christ. He will ultimately be defeated and cast into the Lake of Fire, where the Antichrist and False Prophet already reside (Revelation 20:7-10).

Finally, the Lord Jesus Christ will summon all unbelievers from throughout history before His Great White Throne (Revelation 20:11-15), marking the final judgment. All present will be unsaved and cast into the Lake of Fire.

God will then create a *"new heavens and a new earth,"* marking the beginning of the Eternal Day (Revelation 21:1-22:4; Isaiah 65:17; 66:22; 2 Peter 3:13).

CHAPTER 12

THE CONCERN OF CERN

CERN: Pioneering Particle Physics and Its Significance

The European Organization for Nuclear Research, or CERN, is a premier center for particle physics established in 1954 near Geneva, Switzerland. Its location fosters international collaboration, uniting scientists from over 100 countries. The site is geologically stable, crucial for the operation of the Large Hadron Collider (LHC), the world's largest particle accelerator.

CERN's mission is to explore the universe's fundamental nature. The LHC accelerates protons to near light speed, enabling studies of particle collisions, leading to significant discoveries like the Higgs boson in 2012. CERN's advancements in particle detection also have medical applications, such as in cancer therapy, and it contributed to the creation of the World Wide Web. The Shiva statue at CERN represents the Hindu deity known as the "Destroyer," symbolizing the cyclical nature of creation and destruction. It serves as a metaphor for the scientific exploration of the universe, particularly in particle physics, where particles are created and

Annihilated in experiments, the statue reflects the idea that through destruction, new knowledge and understanding can emerge.

Some interpretations suggest a connection between CERN and the biblical figure Apollyon, the destroyer, as referenced in Revelation 9:1-11, where a fallen star opens the Abyss, releasing locusts with the power to harm.

"And they were told not to harm the grass of the earth or any green plant or any tree, but only those people who do not have the seal of God on their foreheads. They were allowed to torment them for five months, but not to kill them, and their torment was like the torment of a scorpion when it stings someone." (Revelation 9:4-5)

This passage depicts a vivid and symbolic representation of the locusts released from the abyss, emphasizing the suffering they cause to those who do not belong to God. The research conducted at CERN, particularly in high-energy physics, raises questions about the potential consequences of manipulating fundamental forces of nature.

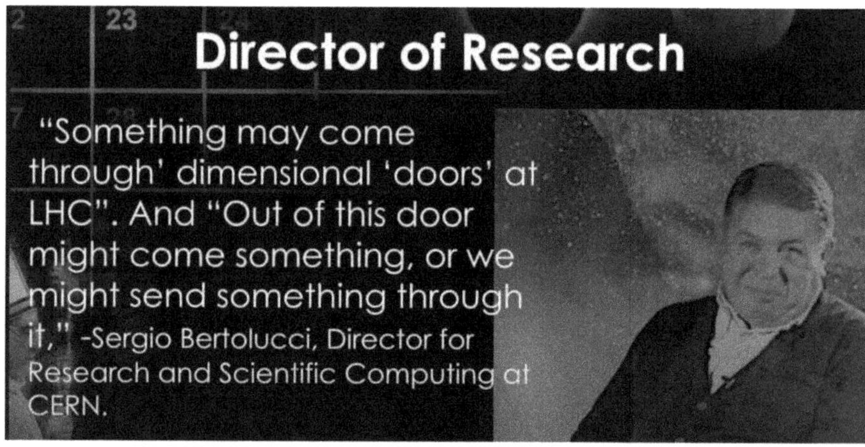

Moving forward, CERN plans to upgrade the LHC with the High-Luminosity Large Hadron Collider (HL-LHC) by the late 2020s, which will allow for deeper investigations into phenomena like dark matter. There are also proposals for a Future Circular Collider (FCC) to further explore fundamental questions about the universe.

CHAPTER 13

THE GREAT RESET

The Great Reset: A Pathway to Global Control

Introduction

In a contemporary world increasingly characterized by intricate global challenges, a compelling narrative has emerged from influential institutions such as the World Economic Forum (WEF). This narrative introduces a controversial initiative known as the Great Reset. This ambitious endeavor envisions a future in which individuals are led to believe they will "own nothing and be happy." However, a growing legion of critics contends that this vision resembles a form of global communism rather than aligning with the cherished ideals of personal freedom and individual rights.

When scrutinized through the lens of the United Nations' Agenda 2030 and the World Health Organization (WHO), the Great Reset appears to be a crucial component of a broader strategy aimed at establishing a centralized world government by the year 2030. Coupled with the contentious handling of the COVID-19 pandemic—widely regarded by skeptics as a manufactured crisis—and the prevailing narrative surrounding man-made climate change, this chapter will delve into these interconnected themes and investigate the implications of central bank digital currencies (CBDCs) as potential instruments of global control. Additionally, the initiative's focus on diversity, equity, and inclusion (DEI) will be examined to reveal how these principles serve to further the overarching agenda. Ultimately, this framework raises concerns about the possibility of an economic disaster that could pave the way for a new system in which the Antichrist could emerge and rule the world, potentially enforcing the infamous mark of the beast.

The Great Reset: A Blueprint for Control

The Great Reset was officially unveiled by the WEF in June 2020, framing the COVID-19 pandemic as a unique opportunity to rethink and reshape our economies and societies. The provocative phrase "you will own nothing, and you will be happy" encapsulates a vision where...

Traditional notions of ownership and individual property are discarded in favor of shared resources and communal living arrangements. While such ideas can be articulated in the alluring language of sustainability and social equity, they raise profound concerns about individual autonomy and economic freedom.

Critics assert that this plan is a thinly veiled attempt to implement a global communist framework—one in which the state, rather than the individual, exerts control over resources and dictates the distribution of wealth. The seductive promise of happiness in a world where ownership is rendered obsolete is perceived as a deceptive illusion, obscuring the harsh reality of increased dependency on government systems. By promoting a narrative that diminishes personal responsibility and ownership, the Great Reset could pave the way for a society where individuals find themselves subjected to the whims of a centralized authority, stripped of their rights and freedoms.

Agenda 2030 and the Quest for Global Governance

The United Nations' Agenda 2030, established in 2015, outlines 17 Sustainable Development Goals (SDGs) aimed at addressing urgent global issues such as poverty, inequality, and environmental sustainability. While these goals may appear noble at first glance, they are criticized for their potential to undermine national sovereignty and individual liberties. The alignment of Agenda 2030 with the principles of the Great Reset suggests a coordinated effort to establish a centralized global governance structure that could override local decision-making and impose uniform policies on nations worldwide.

The role of the WHO in this overarching framework is particularly troubling, as...

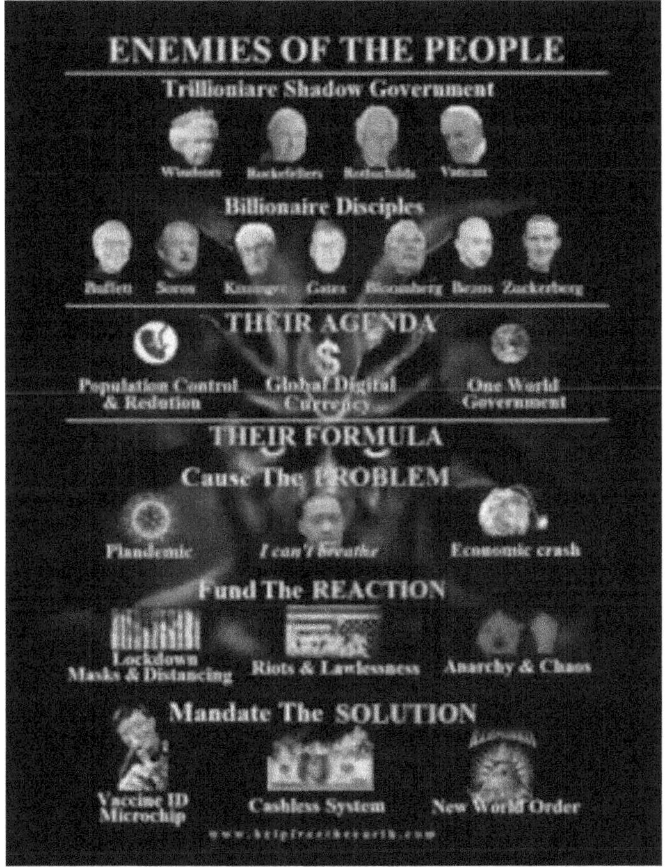

The organization advocates for harmonized health policies and practices across nations. The COVID-19 pandemic has been utilized as a justification for fostering greater cooperation and control over public health, leading many to express concerns about the erosion of local governance and individual rights.

This trajectory raises critical questions about the extent to which global organizations will dictate health and lifestyle choices in the name of public welfare and safety.

The COVID-19 Pandemic: A Manufactured Crisis?

The COVID-19 pandemic has undeniably transformed the global landscape, but many skeptics assert that the narrative surrounding it has been deliberately manipulated to further the objectives of the Great Reset and Agenda 2030. Critics contend that the pandemic was not merely a natural public health crisis but rather a manufactured crisis, engineered to instill fear and justify authoritarian measures. The rapid implementation of lockdowns, vaccine mandates, and intrusive surveillance systems has resulted in widespread apprehension regarding government overreach and the degradation of civil liberties.

This perspective posits that the pandemic served as a strategic opportunity for globalists to advance their agenda, exploiting the fear generated by the virus to promote acceptance of radical changes in governance and economic structures. Detractors argue that the pandemic narrative functions not only as a public health issue but also as a means to condition the populace for a future in which individual freedoms are sacrificed for the sake of collective safety and control.

Man-Made Climate Change: A Convenient Justification

In tandem with the COVID-19 narrative, the discourse surrounding man-made climate change has also gained prominence as a justification for extensive governmental intervention. The assertion that human activity is driving catastrophic climate change has been leveraged to promote policies that prioritize environmental sustainability over economic growth.

However, skeptics argue that this narrative is frequently exaggerated, serving as a pretext for implementing policies that restrict personal freedoms while expanding governmental control. The push for radical measures to combat climate change aligns closely with the principles of the Great Reset, in which economic systems are restructured under...

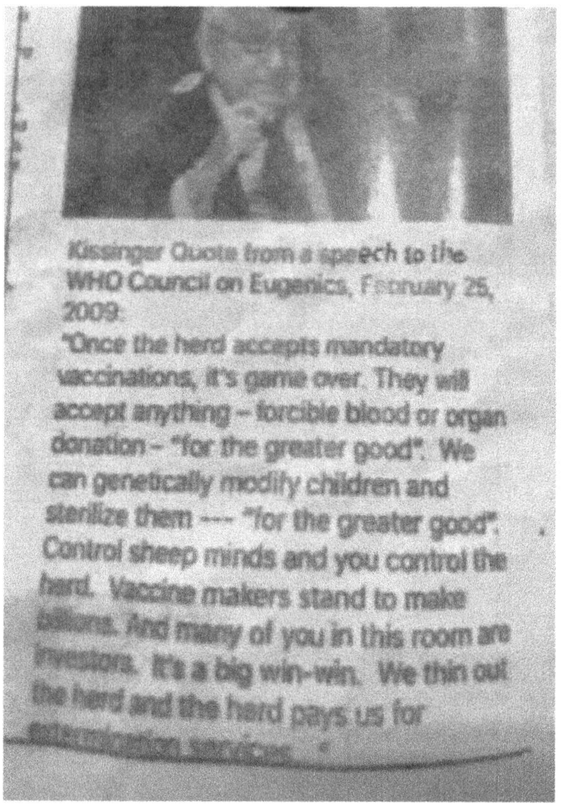

the guise of environmental responsibility. Critics contend that this creates a paradox: while claiming to protect the planet, these measures may inadvertently lead to greater economic disparity and diminished individual autonomy. The narrative surrounding climate change thus becomes another tool in the arsenal of those advocating for centralized control.

Hitler's close confidant, the industrialist and fascist "Eugen Schwab" was in charge of "Escher-Wyss" and had his own concentration camp where prisoners had to work for free. They owned nothing and I suspect were bloody miserable. Klaus is an apple from the same tree.

5:00 AM · May 24, 2022

Central Bank Digital Currencies: The Final Frontier of Control

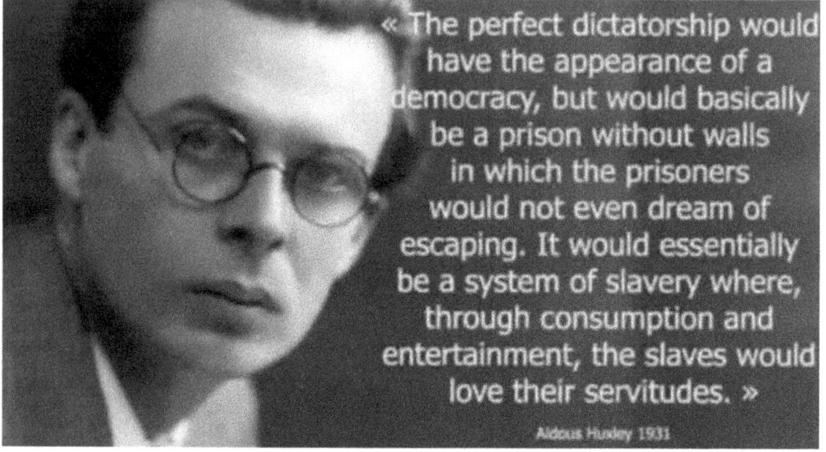

One of the most alarming developments emerging from this global agenda is the growing push for central bank digital currencies (CBDCs). Proponents argue that CBDCs can modernize financial transactions and enhance economic efficiency. However, critics warn that these digital currencies could become the ultimate tool for government surveillance and control over individuals' financial lives.

With CBDCs, governments would possess the capacity to monitor and regulate every transaction, potentially imposing restrictions based on behavioral criteria. This level of oversight raises significant concerns regarding privacy and freedom, as citizens could find themselves operating within a system where their financial autonomy is severely compromised. The integration of CBDCs into the framework of the Great Reset signals a future in which personal financial transactions are subject to scrutiny and control by a centralized authority, raising alarms about the erosion of individual rights.

Diversity, Equity, and Inclusion: A Tool for Compliance

An essential aspect of the Great Reset is its emphasis on diversity, equity, and inclusion (DEI). While these principles are often championed as pathways to social justice and equality, critics argue that they function as mechanisms for enforcing conformity and suppressing dissenting viewpoints. The promotion of DEI initiatives may create an environment where adherence to specific ideological perspectives is expected, stifling open dialogue and critical thinking.

In the context of the Great Reset, the integration of DEI into corporate and governmental policies can be interpreted as a means to further consolidate control. By prioritizing group identity over individual merit, the agenda may

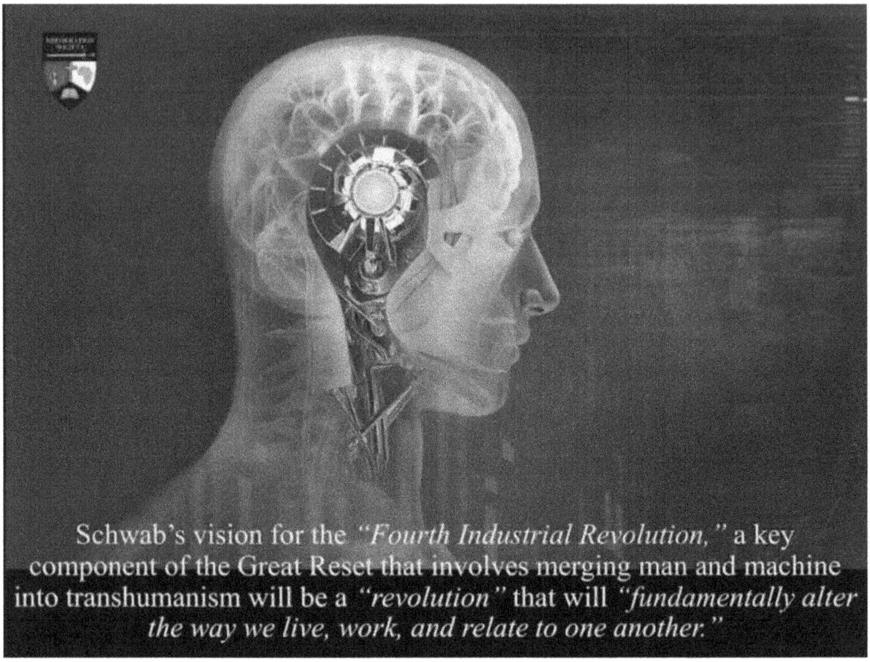

Schwab's vision for the *"Fourth Industrial Revolution,"* a key component of the Great Reset that involves merging man and machine into transhumanism will be a *"revolution"* that will *"fundamentally alter the way we live, work, and relate to one another."*

Inadvertently create divisions within society, undermining the very unity it purports to promote. This focus on DEI can become a tool for enforcing compliance with the broader goals of the Great Reset, compelling individuals to align with a specific set of values or risk exclusion from societal benefits.

SEPTEMBER 14, 2022 · 1 HR 32 MIN

Government Creating a 'Luciferase' Mark to Track Vaccinations; CDC Admits Myocarditis Risk

CrossroadsET

▶ Play

The Potential for Economic Disaster and the Rise of the Antichrist

As the Great Reset unfolds, concerns arise regarding the potential for an economic disaster that could serve as a precursor to a new system of control. The radical restructuring of economies and the imposition of central bank digital currencies may lead to unprecedented financial instability. This upheaval could create the conditions necessary for a new world order—a system in which a singular, authoritarian figure, often referred to as the Antichrist, could rise to power.

In this dystopian vision, the Antichrist could establish dominion over the global populace, utilizing mechanisms such as the proposed mark of the beast to enforce compliance and eliminate dissent. The frightening prospect of a world where individuals are compelled to accept a digital identifier to participate in economic life raises alarm bells for those who value individual freedom and autonomy. In this scenario, the convergence of the Great Reset, Agenda 2030, and the push for CBDCs could culminate in a society where personal liberties are sacrificed at the altar of collective control, enabling a figure of immense power to dictate the terms of existence for all.

Conclusion

The Great Reset, when viewed in conjunction with the UN's Agenda 2030 and the narratives surrounding the COVID-19 pandemic and climate change, represents a complex web of global ambitions that warrants thorough and critical examination. While the stated goals may resonate with ideals of sustainability, social equity, and inclusion, the implications for individual freedoms and national sovereignty are profound and deeply troubling. As the world stands on the precipice of potential shifts toward central bank digital currencies and heightened governmental control, it is imperative for citizens to critically assess the narratives propagated by powerful organizations. The future of global governance is at a pivotal juncture, and the choices made today could ultimately determine whether individual rights and freedoms are preserved or surrendered to a centralized power.

It is essential that the conversation shifts toward transparency, accountability, and the safeguarding of personal liberties in the face of encroaching authoritarianism, ensuring that the future remains in the hands of the many rather than the few. The pursuit of a more equitable society must not come at the expense of the fundamental rights that underpin true freedom and democracy.

CHAPTER 14

MYSTERY BABYLON

Mystery Babylon: Unraveling the Identity of the United States in Revelation

The Book of Revelation, a profound narrative filled with apocalyptic imagery and intricate symbolism, has intrigued scholars, theologians, and curious minds alike for generations. One of its most provocative figures is "Mystery Babylon," commonly interpreted as a representation of moral decay, rampant materialism, and spiritual degradation. Although the United States of America is not explicitly referenced in the sacred texts, many contend that the similarities between this nation and the attributes of Mystery Babylon are both compelling and concerning. This chapter seeks to delve into the defining characteristics of Mystery Babylon, analyze the socioeconomic and cultural landscape of the United States, and argue that the connection between the two is not only plausible but also deeply alarming.

PROPHECY ABOUT MYSTERY BABYLON

YAHUAH is against Mystery Babylon!
By reviewing what He says in regard to Babylon you will be able to properly
determine that the United States of America is Mystery Babylon.

CHARACTERISTICS OF MYSTERY BABYLON

- Mystery Babylon is a nation, not a system *(Jeremiah 50:12)*
- Babylon has a mother that bore her and her mother will be ashamed *(Jeremiah 50:12)*
- Babylon will reap the wrath of YAHUAH *(Jeremiah 50:13)*
- Babylon has sinned against YAHUAH *(Jeremiah 50:14, 24)*
- Babylon was the hammer of the whole earth *(Jeremiah 50:23)*
- She has been proud against YAHUAH *(Jeremiah 50:29)*
- YAHUAH is against Babylon *(Jeremiah 50:31)*
- Babylon will be called the "Lady of Kingdom's" *(Isaiah 47:5)*
- Babylon will have a drought *(Jeremiah 50:38)*
- Babylon is a land of carved images *(Jeremiah 50:38)*
- Babylon is insane with their idols *(Jeremiah 50:38)*
- The other nations in the world are drunk off her wine, or deeply influenced by her *(Jeremiah 51:7, Revelation 18:3)*
- There are people who live in Babylon that originate from other countries *(Jeremiah 51:9)*
- Babylon is located around many waters *(Jeremiah 51:13)*
- Babylon is abundant in treasures *(Jeremiah 51:13)*
- Babylon tried to get up to heaven *(Jeremiah 51:53)*
- Babylon becomes a dwelling place of demons. It is a prison for every foul spirit. It is a cage for every unclean and hated bird. *(Revelation 18:2)*
- The businessmen of the earth become rich from Babylon's abundance *(Revelation 18:3)*
- Babylon glorified herself and lived luxuriously *(Revelation 18:7)*
- Other kings and rulers of the earth will have become rich and lived luxuriously because of her *(Revelation 18:9)*
- The businessman will weep because they can't do business the same anymore *(Revelation 18:11)*
- Babylon will have a great city that allowed others to become rich because of her wealth *(Revelation 18:19)*
- Babylon's businessmen were the great men of the earth *(Revelation 18:23)*
- From their sorcery, Babylon's businessmen deceived the whole earth *(Revelation 18:23)*
- There is a lot of sorcery and enchantments going on in Babylon *(Isaiah 47:9)*
- Babylon will be the youngest of nations *(Jeremiah 50:12)*
- Babylon will be the center of the world *(Revelation 18:3)*
- Babylon uses astrology, sorcerers, and mystics for guidance *(Isaiah 47:13, Revelation 18:2)*

truthunedited.com

JUDGEMENT AGAINST BABYLON

* Babylon's idols will be humiliated and her images will be broken in pieces *(Jeremiah 50:2)*
* All that take part in Babylon's plundering will be satisfied *(Jeremiah 50:10)*
* YAH allows others to take out vengeance on Babylon *(Jeremiah 50:14-15, 25-27,29)*
* Babylon's young men will fall in the streets *(Jeremiah 50:30)*
* It will be overthrown like Sodom & Gomorrah *(Jeremiah 50:40)*
* When Babylon is taken, the earth trembles and a cry is heard from other nations *(Jeremiah 50:46)*
* Babylon will have a day of doom *(Jeremiah 51:2)*
* Babylon will fall and be destroyed *(Jeremiah 51:8)*
* YAHUAH will take vengeance upon Babylon. *(Jeremiah 51:11)*
* YAH's plan is to destroy Babylon *(Jeremiah 51:11)*
* Babylon's plagues will come in one day *(Revelation 18:8)*
* Babylon's judgement will come in one hour *(Revelation 18:10, 17, 19)*

BABYLON WILL BE ATTACKED

* A nation from the north will attack Babylon *(Jeremiah 50:3,41)*
* Babylon's land will become desolate and inhabitable for both man & animals *(Jeremiah 50:3,13,39,41)*
* YAHUAH will cause many nations from the north to assemble and attack Babylon *(Jeremiah 50:9, 51:6)*
* Babylon will be plundered *(Jeremiah 50:10)*
* Babylon's army will be cut off *(Jeremiah 50:30)*

BABYLON & ISRAEL

* Babylon carried away Hebrew slaves into captivity *(Jeremiah 52:28-30)*
* Many in the church (the assembly) in Babylon will be lost sheep *(Jeremiah 50:6)*
* Pastors & influencers in Babylon will lead the church astray *(Jeremiah 50:6)*
* They don't rest in YAHUAH anymore *(Jeremiah 50:6)*
* The bridegroom & bride will no longer be there *(Revelation 18:23)*

WARNINGS

* Babylon's young men will not be spared *(Jeremiah 51:3)*
* The most proud in Babylon will stumble and fall *(Jeremiah 50:32)*
* There will be fires in the proud's cities and they will devour Babylon *(Jeremiah 50:32)*
* Those that come against Babylon will be cruel and will not show mercy *(Jeremiah 50:42)*
* Come out of Babylon *(Revelation 18:4)*

truthunedited.com

Understanding the Essence of Mystery Babylon

Mystery Babylon is portrayed in Revelation as a grand metropolis, a formidable entity that exerts significant influence over global powers. It is characterized by its extravagant wealth, moral corruption, and idolatrous practices. Revelation 17 refers to it as "the mother of harlots," suggesting a profound level of depravity that extends beyond mere political or economic power. This entity is also associated with the persecution of the faithful, embodying an ethos that stands in stark opposition to divine principles and celebrates excess and indulgence.

The vivid imagery surrounding Mystery Babylon paints a troubling portrait of a society that has forsaken spiritual truths in favor of material gain and hedonistic pleasures. This central theme reverberates throughout the text, issuing dire warnings about the inevitable consequences that accompany such a lifestyle—a downfall that is often depicted as both swift and catastrophic.

Chapter 17
is talking of the whore of Babylon, a religious entity

The United States - A Contemporary Reflection

When examining the United States through the lens of the characteristics commonly attributed to Mystery Babylon, the parallels become increasingly evident. First and foremost, the United States functions as a global superpower, wielding substantial influence over international politics and economics. Its formidable military strength and economic capabilities enable it to dominate the global arena, mirroring the reign of Mystery Babylon over the rulers of the earth.

Chapter 18
is dealing with a governmental entity

Culturally, the U.S. exports a way of life that is frequently characterized by consumerism and individualism. From the glitz of Hollywood to the allure of fast fashion, American culture promotes values that often prioritize personal satisfaction at the expense of communal well-being. This relentless pursuit of material wealth and social status aligns closely with the biblical admonitions against idolatry and moral decay. The omnipresence of American consumer culture can be viewed as a modern-day reflection of the spiritual emptiness described in Revelation.

Economically, the United States epitomizes the extremes of wealth and poverty, functioning within a capitalist framework that tends to reward excess while neglecting the needs of the less fortunate. This glaring economic disparity mirrors the decadence associated with Mystery Babylon, wherein the affluent continue to amass wealth, often at the expense of the marginalized and disenfranchised. The unyielding drive for profit, irrespective of ethical considerations, resonates with the warnings found in Revelation regarding the dire repercussions of unchecked avarice.

The Moral and Spiritual Landscape

The moral landscape of contemporary America also raises significant concerns that reflect the depiction of Mystery Babylon. Over recent decades, there has been a notable and concerning shift toward secularism, accompanied by a gradual decline in traditional moral values. The normalization of behaviors once deemed unacceptable, and the diminishing sway of religious institutions signify a potential departure from the Judeo-Christian foundations that many argue are critical for a healthy and thriving society.

Moreover, the increasing persecution of individuals and communities who uphold conventional moral standards highlights a growing rift within society. Those who advocate for Judeo-Christian principles frequently find themselves at odds with a culture that increasingly embraces relativism and moral ambiguity. This tension mirrors the biblical narrative of the faithful being oppressed and marginalized, further reinforcing the connection between the United States and the characteristics of Mystery Babylon.

In summary, while the United is not directly mentioned within the pages of the Book of Revelation, the correlation between this nation and the figure of Mystery Babylon is undeniably striking. Through its political supremacy, cultural influence, economic excesses, and moral decline, the U.S. embodies many of the attributes associated with this enigmatic entity. The warnings embedded within Revelation serve as a cautionary tale, urging contemporary society to reflect critically on its values and choices. As the United States continues to navigate the complexities and challenges of modern life, the lessons of Mystery Babylon resonate with profound relevance, calling for introspection and a return to more grounded, spiritually attuned principles. The implications of these parallels are significant, challenging us to contemplate the trajectory of our society such as moral and economic decline as well the potential consequences of nuclear war.

CHAPTER 15

JESUS IS COMING VERY SOON

"Look, I am coming soon! My reward is with me, and I will give to each person according to what they have done" (Revelation 22:12).

God promises crowns as rewards for faithfulness and service. Here are seven different crowns mentioned in scripture, along with a brief description of each:

1. The Crown of Life: Mentioned in James 1:12 and Revelation 2:10, this crown is promised to those who endure trials, temptations, and persecution for their faith. It signifies eternal life and the reward for steadfastness in the face of adversity.

2. The Incorruptible Crown: Found in 1 Corinthians 9:24-25, this crown is awarded to those who exercise self-control and discipline in their spiritual lives. It symbolizes the reward for running the race of faith with perseverance and dedication.

3. The Crown of Righteousness: In 2 Timothy 4:7-8, the Apostle Paul speaks of this crown, which is given to those who long for the return of Jesus Christ. It represents the righteousness that

comes from faith and the hope of eternal life, particularly for those who eagerly await Christ's second coming.

4. The Crown of Glory: This crown is mentioned in 1 Peter 5:2-4 and is specifically for leaders and shepherds who guide and care for God's people. It signifies the reward for faithful service and the responsibility of spiritual leadership.

5. The Crown of Rejoicing: Found in 1 Thessalonians 2:19-20, this crown is often referred to as the soul-winner's crown. It is given to those who bring others to Christ, reflecting the joy and fulfillment of participating in God's redemptive work.

6. The Crown of Faith: Although not explicitly named in scripture, this crown is associated with the faithfulness of believers throughout their lives. It represents the reward for maintaining faith in God and trusting in His promises.

7. The Crown for Looking for His Appearing: Specifically tied to the expectation of Christ's return, this crown is associated with those who live in anticipation of the second coming of Jesus.While it is often linked with the "Crown of Righteousness," it emphasizes the importance of hope and readiness for the return of the Lord.

1 Thessalonians 5:2-4. It states:

"For you yourselves are fully aware that the day of the Lord will come like a thief in the night. While people are saying, 'There is peace and security,' then sudden destruction will come upon them as labor pains come upon a pregnant woman, and they will not escape. But you are not in darkness, brothers, for that day to surprise you like a thief." (ESV)

In this passage, the Apostle Paul emphasizes that while the day of the Lord may come unexpectedly for those who are not vigilant, believers— described as "not in darkness"—should be aware and prepared for Christ's return.

So in closing, I hope this book helps you prepare in these last moments for the Lords return. Now more than ever, we the last generation should be giving our final push whether it's ministry, giving or self-purification. Just like running a race when you see the finish line, you sprint as hard as you can because you know times up!

Psalm 83 War will lead to the annihilation of Israel's neighbors; rather, it will subdue them, rendering them incapable of posing a threat. This belief is rooted in the scriptural understanding that Jesus Christ will ultimately judge some of these nations upon His return.

ARE
YOU
READY?

SO MUCH MORE

There is so much more that I could unpack in this book regarding censorship, the manipulation of truth, depopulation, the proliferation of untested vaccines, and the brink of devastating wars. However, I have concluded that this is not the space for such discussions. My purpose with this book is to sound the alarm that Christ is coming very, very soon—indeed, at the door.

1. 1 Thessalonians 5:2-3 (NIV): "For you know very well that the day of the Lord will come like a thief in the night. While people are saying, 'Peace and safety,' destruction will come on them suddenly, as labor pains on a pregnant woman, and they will not escape."

2. 2 Peter 3:10 (NIV): "But the day of the Lord will come like a thief. The heavens will disappear with a roar; the elements will be destroyed by fire, and the earth and everything done in it will be laid bare."

Revelation 3:3 (NIV): "Remember, therefore, what you have received and heard; hold it fast, and repent. But if you do not wake up, I will come like a thief, and you will not know at what time I will come to you."

Revelation 16:15 (NIV): "Look, I come like a thief! Blessed is the one who stays awake and remains clothed, so as not to go naked and be shamefully exposed."

However, to those of us that diligently look for his signs, it won't be unexpected to us. Everyone should have an eternal perspective because it will change your whole outlook on life and prioritize what's most important and give you a new reason to live. With the coming events that are about to take place in the world, I would be very surprised to still be waiting for Christ in 2025, but then again only Jesus knows.

Jesus told us that when we see these signs beginning to take place, we should "lift up your heads, because your redemption draws near" (Luke 21:28).

For those that are interested in world events that are heavily censored because of their evil agenda and not meant to be available on mainstream platforms so as to hide their evil nature, go to stopworldcontrol.com. David Sorensen has done an amazing job of uncovering the evil in our world today. Although he doesn't comprehend God's future for humanity correctly, his work is nonetheless excellent.

ABOUT THE AUTHOR

Darren Shirley, born in 1969 in Edmonton, Canada, moved to Mexico in 1997. My parents and sister followed me to Puerto Vallarta in 2004. I have two children born here with my first wife and got remarried in 2018 to Lanoi. I began to take an interest in Bible prophecy when I was 14, which led me to be saved when I was 16. Since then, it has been my passion to share my insights with anyone who has ears to hear. It is my hope that this book will also inspire others to spread the message of Christ's imminent return, leading them to His salvation and glorious kingdom.

FINAL THOUGHTS

When I was a child, I was very interested in making mazes. I would practice creating them at a very high level of difficulty. I used to take them to school so my teacher could make copies for all the classmates, and they would often frustrate them, with only one or two figuring them out in time. I even had the class bully tell me it couldn't be done, so I had to show him how, or it would have ended in a fight. Reflecting on this, it reminds me of how my life has been like a maze. Many times, I thought I was going the right way, only to end up at a dead end. It wasn't until recently that I found the way out of this crazy maze of life and now am sober and clear-minded about the truth.

I want to thank my wife, Lanoi, who is the most amazing, beautiful, compassionate, and strong woman I've ever met. Without her support and love, these last several years would have been much more difficult. Thank you for everything. Praise God!

For further communication, I can be reached at livingpv@gmail.com